THE PROPHETS
and
THE POWERLESS

JAMES LIMBURG

JOHN KNOX PRESS
ATLANTA

To my teacher
John Bright

LIBRARY OF CONGRESS CATALOGING IN PUBLICATION DATA

Limburg, James, 1935–
    The prophets and the powerless.

    Bibliography: p.
    1. Prophets. 2. Prophecy. I. Title.
BS1198.L5   220.1′5   76–12397
ISBN 0–8042–0156–0

Copyright © 1977 John Knox Press
Atlanta, Georgia
Printed in the U.S.A.

Preface

This book is being written in response to two conversations. The first was with the pastor of the congregation to which our family belongs. He cornered me after services one Sunday to ask if I would give some lectures on the prophets. "There is a new interest in prophecy these days," he said. "People are coming to us with all sorts of questions, particularly after reading books like *The Late Great Planet Earth*, and are wondering what the prophets really have to say." As a college teacher of the Old Testament, and with something of a guilty conscience for not having been out on the firing lines as a Sunday School teacher for a while, I could hardly say no.

The second conversation also took place at the church, but this time with a boy of perhaps ten years. I don't know his name, but I found him outside the door one Sunday morning. He had obviously just come from Sunday School class and was waiting for someone, standing there with a black Bible clutched in his hand. Since I was waiting, too, I engaged him in casual conversation.

"Just come from Sunday School?" I asked.

"Yup," he said.

"What are you studying?" I said.

"The Old Testament," he answered. Then I became interested.

"And how do you like it?" I asked in all innocence, expecting perhaps a pearl of wisdom from this obviously alert young fellow, maybe confirming my notion that anyone of any age who gets into the actual texts of the Old Testament is bound to find the material quite exciting.

"Boring," was his reply. Then he left to meet his mother, and I was left with one less theory about teaching the Bible to ten-year-olds.

The pastor was right. There is a new interest in prophecy these days. Walk into a bookstore, or look over the paperback collection in the local drugstore, and you'll find titles like, *A Gift of Prophecy*, *My Life and Prophecies*, *The Call to Glory: Jeane Dixon Speaks of Jesus and Prophecy*, all concerning that lady who lives in Washington, D.C. Next to these books you might discover, *Edgar Cayce—The Sleeping Prophet*, plus a dozen or so more books about that interesting fellow who lived in Virginia and died there in 1945. A number of books offer interpretations of the biblical prophets. Erich von Däniken's international best-seller, *Chariots of the Gods?* argues that references to spaceships and astronauts may be found in the book of Ezekiel. A spin-off by another author is entitled, *The Spaceships of Ezekiel*. Then there is Hal Lindsey's, *The Late Great Planet Earth*, advertising itself as "a penetrating look at incredible prophecies involving this generation," as well as his more recent *There's a New World Coming*, identified as "A Prophetic Odyssey."[1] What are we to make of these figures called "prophets," who use crystal balls, get into trances, or make alarming predictions? What of these biblical interpreters who find spaceships in Ezekiel and offer detailed maps of military maneuvers in the Middle East? And all claim, somehow, to be related to biblical prophecy. Little wonder that the layman is confused!

But that ten year old boy was right, too. He gave an unambiguous instant critique of much of our Bible teaching in the church: not heretical or even unorthodox, just "boring"! Why is it that the very announcement of a "Bible Study" triggers in that boy's parents the yawn, glance at the watch, "Haven't we got something else on for Wednesday evening?"

kind of reaction? Isn't it because while our teaching may be related to the biblical texts, it has been unrelated to life, and is therefore dull? And now suddenly we have a whole shelf full of books about prophecy which are excitingly written and seem to relate to life, but which have little or no relationship to what the prophets actually have to say!

What can we do in such a situation? To begin with, it would seem that boredom with Bible study is not the real problem, but rather a symptom of a deeper problem. The real problem is not with the words of the prophets. We can be sure that no one ever described the preaching of Amos or Jeremiah as boring! Individuals are not ordered out of the country (Amos 7:12) for mouthing pious irrelevancies, nor are they nearly lynched (Jer. 26:11) for delivering harmless homilies. Nor should we think that the problem is with people today. One suspects that despite the differences between the time of Isaiah and our own time, people have not really changed so much.

If the reason for boredom with the Bible is not connected with the words of the prophets nor with the people of today, then it must have something to do with the way in which the gap between prophetic word and contemporary hearer is bridged. In other words, the real problem is one of interpretation, or hermeneutics. The purpose of this book is to help you in interpreting the prophets, to assist you in learning how to listen to what they have to say. We shall outline a simple method of interpretation (Chapter 2) and then offer some illustrations of that method (Chapters 4–6). As you learn how to interpret the prophetic texts, we shall hope that you will begin to discover for yourself why synagogue and church have always heard in the words of the prophets a Word from God.

But why this theme, "The Prophets and the Powerless"? We might come to the prophets with all sorts of questions about the end of the world, the way of salvation, or the nature of God. We may even be so sophisticated as to frame these questions in terms of eschatology, soteriology, and theology. But the prophets keep surprising us. Time and again they take us by the hand and lead us to the home of a widow or point us to a lonely orphan. They may show us the eyes of a poor man, or introduce us to a stranger. These, you see, are the powerless. Such encounters always leave us a bit uncomfortable, and we become even more uncomfortable when we hear the prophets say that true religion has something to do with these folks. This is not the only theme in the preaching of the prophets. But it is a central one, and a good place to begin.

Finally, a word about the dedication. One of the pieces of advice in the Talmud is, "Find yourself a teacher . . . " (*Pirke Abot*). A great many of us have found in Professor John Bright of Union Theological Seminary in Virginia a teacher who has inspired, instructed, and encouraged us in our study of the Old Testament. This book is dedicated to him, with continuing gratitude.

James Limburg

Contents

1

What Was a Prophet?

During the past year, our town has been visited by a number of individuals identified in the local press as "prophets." One took out a good-sized advertisement which began, "I want to personally invite you to a special PROPHECY BANQUET . . . " The speaker promised to deal with questions like, "Is the Antichrist alive today?" and "Are the End-Time nations already formed?" He would make predictions on everything from a coming water crisis to "Your future . . . five years from now!" A bit later, the newspaper announced the coming of a singer and guitarist "widely acclaimed as a modern day prophet through the use of music." And then there were a number of full-page advertisements concerning the visit of a Korean, who would speak "with prophetic insight into the new future of Christianity."

But what does it mean to call someone a "prophet" today? We can use the term loosely, to denote one who speaks out for a cause, speculates on the future, or even for someone who predicts the weather! We are interested, however, in a more restricted use of the term. What does it mean to call someone a prophet in the biblical sense? To put the question another way, *Are there prophets today who are like the prophets in biblical times*? We shall begin dealing with this question by looking at some individuals of our time who are identified with prophets or prophecy, and by trying to put them in some kind of historical perspective.

SEERS, HOLY MEN, AND DIVINERS

Edgar Cayce (pronounced like "Casey") is called by his biographer "The Sleeping Prophet." He was born in Kentucky in 1877, died in Virginia in 1945, and is described as a sixth-grade dropout, a kindly and religious man who taught Sunday School and who read the Bible every day. For over forty years he gave "readings" while in a trance-like state. He would diagnose illnesses and prescribe cures for people whom he saw only in visions. He predicted future events. Today, tens of thousands of his readings, recorded by his wife and by his secretary, are on file at the Association for Research and Enlightenment in Virginia Beach, Virginia. Over a dozen paperbacks have been published about Cayce, most of them within the past few years, on subjects ranging from food to the Dead Sea Scrolls, the Bible, and Jesus. His biographer reports Cayce's first visionary experience, when he was a boy of seven or eight. He had been reading the Bible in a secluded glade when he saw a figure in white and heard a voice:

" . . . What would you ask of me, that I may give it to you?"

" . . . Just that I may be helpful to others," he replied, "especially to children who are ill, and that I may love my fellow man."[1] Cayce appears to have been a humble man, who said after one dramatic healing, "'I myself have done nothing. I am but a channel of this great gift . . . .'"[2] Edgar Cayce healed, predicted, had visions and unusual experiences. Shall we then call him a prophet, like the biblical prophets?

Jeane Dixon, now living in Washington, D.C., is better known than Edgar Cayce. But in many ways their stories are alike. Her biographer ascribes to Mrs. Dixon a "gift of prophecy," and says that her visions "apparently lift the curtain on tomorrow in much the same manner as did those of Old Testament prophets."[3] She, too, reports an early visionary experience. At the age of eight she visited a gypsy in California, and saw in a crystal ball the ocean and the land from which the gypsy came.[4] Books by and about Mrs. Dixon report a succession of visions and predictions regarding events of personal, national, and international importance. Like Cayce, Mrs. Dixon comes through as a genuine person. Speaking of her predictive ability she says, " 'I believe that I am only an instrument through which these things come, for a purpose.' "[5] "It is my belief that God has given me a gift of prophecy for his own reasons . . . ."[6] Mrs. Dixon sees visions and makes predictions. Should she then be considered a prophet, like the Old Testament prophets?

Perhaps few people outside the Dakotas are familiar with Black Elk, an Indian of the Oglala Sioux Tribe who lived in South Dakota and who died there in 1950. His story is beautifully told in John Neihardt's book, *Black Elk Speaks*. At various points the account of Black Elk is reminiscent of the stories of Edgar Cayce or Jeane Dixon. When he was nine years old, he had a vision in which he saw his people scattered and suffering.[7] Throughout the rest of his life he continued to hear voices, see visions, and heal the sick. Neihardt reports a remarkable experience of what we might call psychic transportation. While Black Elk was traveling in Europe with Buffalo Bill's Wild West Show, he became ill. During his illness, he took a visionary trip back to the Pine Ridge reservation in South Dakota, and accurately described events which were happening there.[8] Black Elk, too, comes through as a humble and godly man. He says,

> Of course it was not I who cured. It was the power from the outer world, and the visions and ceremonies had only made me like a hole through which the power could come to the two-leggeds.[9]

The book concludes with a description of a trip which the author took with the aged Black Elk, to the top of Harney

Peak in the Black Hills. It was a bright and cloudless day, and
the old man said,

> "Something should happen to-day . If I have any power left,
> the thunder beings of the west should hear me when I send a
> voice, and there should be at least a little thunder and a little
> rain."[10]

He prayed, "O make my people live!" And then, reports
Neihardt, it began to rain.

The account of psychic transportation is reminiscent of
an experience which Ezekiel had (Ezek. 8). The effective
prayer for rain reminds the Bible reader of Elijah at Mount
Carmel (1 Kings 18), and the accounts of his healings sound
much like similar acts of prophets like Elijah. The actions and
experiences of Black Elk are quite similar to actions and
experiences of the biblical prophets. Shall we then call him a
prophet, in the biblical sense?

Before dealing with these questions in regard to Cayce,
Dixon, and Black Elk, we shall cite two further examples. The
first furnishes a parallel to Black Elk's "transportation" experience. In his book, *Prophecy in Ancient Israel*, Johannes
Lindblom relates the following story: A group of people had
assembled at a farm in Lapland, and were awaiting the arrival
of a judge for a legal proceeding. It was winter, and the snow
was falling.

> The judge therefore was later than expected, and they were
> growing impatient, wondering why he did not turn up. In the
> cottage by the fire-side sat an old Lapp. People knew that he
> was a diviner, and a man said to him, "You may as well try to
> find out where the judge is." After much begging and praying,
> the Lapp promised to make an attempt. But he wanted to be
> alone, and no one was to disturb him. He went into the back-
> room. As he stayed there for quite a long time, someone
> peeped in through the door-chink. He then saw the Lapp lying
> on the bed, looking like one dead. After a while he came out,
> looking very tired, and merely said, "He will be here in two

hours." Exactly two hours later the judge arrived, took off his fur coat, and greeted those present. But when he saw the Lapp, he was greatly astonished. "How did you come here?" he said. "We met you two hours ago on the Great Swamp and asked you about the way, didn't we?"[11]

Finally, we shall look at an incident involving a seer from ancient Mesopotamia, as reported in the Bible, Numbers 22—24. The Israelites are on their way from Egypt to the promised land, and are encamped in the territory of Moab, just to the east of the Jordan River. Balak, King of Moab, is afraid of these people, and sends messengers to Mesopotamia to secure the services of a famous diviner named Balaam. Paying the proper fee, the messengers ask Balaam to put a curse on these invading Israelites. After a good deal of initial reluctance, the diviner finally arrives in Moab. He requires elaborate preparations, including seven altars, seven bulls, and seven rams. After a sacrifice has been offered, Balaam reports that he has had a vision of the great number of the people of Israel, but that he cannot curse them (Num. 23:7–10)! The same procedure is tried from two other locations, but each time the result is the same; "there is no enchantment against Jacob, no divination against Israel." (23:23) Instead, Balaam pronounces a blessing, "how fair are your tents, O Jacob, your encampments, O Israel!" (24:5) Finally the diviner is informed that his services are no longer needed, and he offers yet another oracle announcing that Israel will be victorious over Moab (24:15–19).

Now it is apparent that figures as diverse as Edgar Cayce, Jeane Dixon, Black Elk, the Lapp diviner, and Balaam all have something in common. They claim to see things others don't see and hear things others don't hear, through visions, dreams, or trances. They may have abilities to heal, to predict the future, to be "transported," or to pronounce words of good or evil (blessing or curse). These individuals are only examples of types of persons with unusual abilities and experiences who have been known throughout history, and through all parts of the world.

Should we then call them prophets? Are they like the great biblical prophets? We shall return to the question at the end of this chapter, after we have looked a bit more closely at just what a biblical prophet really was. For now, we may observe that an individual of this type may be closely tied to the religion of a people and be considered a "Holy Man," like Black Elk. Others may specialize in locating missing persons or blessing and cursing, and may be labelled as "diviners," such as the Lapp and Balaam. But all have in common the claim that they see and hear things not revealed to other men. Thus "seer" is the best term for describing them.

But what is the relationship between the seer and the biblical prophet? According to the Bible, there is a connection between the two. The first book of Samuel reports that Saul's father once sent him to locate some lost asses (1 Sam. 9). When he had no success, Saul's servant suggested that they visit a "man of God" (he might have said "holy man") in the city and ask him for help. They asked for the "seer," who was Samuel. Then an interesting parenthetical note in the text tells us that "seer" was an earlier name for someone who, at the time of the writer, would be called a "prophet." (1 Sam. 9:9) But this man of God and seer named Samuel could also act very much like the later biblical prophets when he anointed a king (1 Sam. 10) and when he delivered a message of bad news to that same king (1 Sam. 15:22 f.). In the figure of Samuel, at the very beginning of the succession of biblical prophets, we see one who was a "seer" (to be consulted about such things as lost asses) but also a prophet, who could deliver a word of doom to the king.

It is true that the biblical prophets often exhibit abilities similar to those associated with the seer. They do see visions, hear voices, predict the future, experience transportation, heal, and pronounce blessings and curses. There is something of the seer in them. But they are more than seers. And there is another figure from the ancient world which provides the most helpful model for understanding them, and for answering our question, What was a prophet?

THE MESSENGER IN THE ANCIENT WORLD

In the time of ancient Israel, the normal means of communication over a distance was by means of a messenger. We have a number of good examples of message sending in the pages of the Old Testament. Consider the scene where King David, anxious about his son Absalom, is waiting for a report on how the battle has been going. The watchman goes up onto the city wall and reports that he sees a runner approaching; from the way he runs, he even knows who the man is. The runner comes before the king and brings good news, "All is well." Then a second runner comes, this time bringing the bad news that Absalom has been killed (2 Sam. 18:24–33).

A second scene involves Jacob and his company, who are about to pass through territory belonging to Jacob's brother, Esau. The two brothers had been at odds with one another since Jacob cheated Esau out of his birthright, and now Jacob is a bit uneasy about how he will be received:

> And Jacob sent messengers before him to Esau his brother in the land of Seir, the country of Edom, instructing them, "Thus you shall say to my lord Esau: Thus says your servant Jacob, 'I have sojourned with Laban, and stayed until now; and I have oxen, asses, flocks, menservants, and maidservants; and I have sent to tell my Lord, in order that I might find favor in your sight.'" (Gen. 32:3–5)

Of interest here is the way in which the messengers were told to introduce their message. When they arrived before Esau, they would begin, "Thus says your servant Jacob."

A third scene is set in the time of the Judges, before there was a king in Israel, and provides an example of message sending between two nations. The Israelites are being harassed by their Ammonite neighbors. They prevail upon a seasoned warrior named Jephthah to be their leader, hoping that he will be able to bring an end to the Ammonite raids. Jephthah first tries to settle the matter by negotiations, sending messengers to the Ammonite king to ask the reason for the attacks. Of interest to us is the account of the second sending of the messengers. When they arrived at the court of the king of Ammon, the text reports that they introduced their message, "Thus says Jephthah . . ." The message concludes, "I therefore have not sinned against you . . . ," the "I" here being the "I" of the message sender, Jephthah (Judges 11:1–28).

Finally, another scene involving international message sending, this one from the time of King Hezekiah and the prophet Isaiah. Sennacherib, King of Assyria, has been campaigning in Judah and is about to attempt to take Jerusalem, the capital city. But he sends three of his officials to try to convince King Hezekiah to surrender Jerusalem without a fight. These three are met by members of Hezekiah's cabinet, and the Assyrian representative says to them:

> "Say to Hezekiah, 'Thus says the great king, the king of Assyria: On what do you rest this confidence of yours? . . . On whom do you now rely, that you have rebelled against me?'" (2 Kings 18:19–20)

He begins a second speech by saying,

> "Hear the word of the great king, the king of Assyria! Thus says the king: 'Do not let Hezekiah deceive you, for he will not be able to deliver you out of my hand.'" (2 Kings 18:28b–29)

Again, we hear the expression "Thus says the great king," and we see that the "I" of the messenger's speech is really the "I" of the message sender.

In considering these examples of message sending, we note the following:

1. The expression "Thus says X" is frequently used to begin the message, with X indicating the message sender.
2. The "I" of the messenger's speech is the "I" of the message sender.
3. The messenger apparently had a degree of freedom in the formulation of the message. The Assyrian representative was told by his king, we might imagine, "Get Hezekiah to stop rebelling and start acting like an obedient Assyrian satellite again!" That was the essence of the message. The actual formulation of the message was the task of the messenger himself. To put it another way, he was more an ambassador than a postman, with his own personality playing a role in the formulation of the message.
4. The authority for the message lay with the message sender. The messenger in the ancient world, like our modern day ambassador, was given a certain respect and granted a certain protection, because of the one whom he represented.

Perhaps a simple illustration at this point will help to clarify the position of the messenger. I recall trying to work in my study one evening, but being disturbed by the efforts of our daughter upstairs at the piano. I asked our youngest son to run up and tell his sister to stop playing. I heard the footsteps go up, but then come back down, with no change in the music. "She won't stop," said Paul. Then I said, "You go up and tell her that *I said* she should stop playing, and right now!" Now the four-year-old no longer appeared in the role of a harmless little brother, but as a duly commissioned representative of a somewhat higher power. When he said, "Daddy says, 'Stop playing the piano . . . ' " (Thus says the father!), the music stopped, because now the messenger spoke as one who had been given some authority.

A MESSENGER FROM GOD

But what has this to do with the prophets? As we listen to their voices, we hear one expression repeated time and again. When Amos preached his sermon against Israel's neighbors, and then against Israel, he began each new section with "Thus says the Lord." (Amos 1:3, 6, 9, 11, 13; 2:1, 4, 6) We hear the same formula in the preaching of Isaiah (7:7; 10:24; 22:15), Jeremiah (2:2, 5; 4:3; 6:16), Ezekiel (2:4; 3:11; 5:5) and with some variations, throughout the prophetic books. We recognize this "Thus says the Lord" as the "Thus says X" formula used by the messenger in the ancient world. The prophet appears in the role of *messenger*, a messenger from God. The "I" of his messages is very often the "I" of the message sender, the Lord himself. While the message originates with God and is communicated to the prophet in the mystery of inspiration, the form which it eventually takes when delivered to the people appears to be left up to the prophet himself.

As messenger from God, the prophet was more an ambassador than a postman! And like an ambassador, he enjoyed a certain respect and protection, because he represented a power greater than himself. Thus a prophet like Nathan, for example, could walk into the court of the king and accuse David of murder and adultery. What gave Nathan this kind of authority? His only credentials were the "Thus says the Lord" (2 Sam. 12:7) which identified him as a messenger from God (2 Sam. 12). Or Jeremiah could stand in Jerusalem, accuse the citizenry of breaking God's commandments, and then announce that the temple was going to be destroyed (Jer. 7:1–15 and Jer. 26). This sounded very much like both heresy and treason, and we might have expected a lynching. But the prophet was given a trial. His accusers said, " 'This man deserves the sentence of death, because he has prophesied against this city.' " (Jer. 26:11) His only defense was, " 'The LORD sent me,' " (Jer. 26:12–15) and the political leaders recognized that the messenger of God had the right to deliver the message entrusted to him: " 'This man does not deserve the sentence of death, for he has spoken to us in the name of the LORD our God.' " (Jer 26:16)

Now to deal with the question which furnishes the title for this chapter: What was a prophet? Visions, auditions, extraordinary actions and experiences were not foreign to the biblical prophet. There was something of the seer in him. But he was much more a messenger, who had "stood in the council of the LORD" (Jer. 23:18) and who had been commissioned by his Lord to deliver a word to his people. The prophet was a messenger from God.

Are there prophets today? What are we to make of individuals like Black Elk, Edgar Cayce, or Jeane Dixon? For now, we suggest that it is neither accurate nor helpful to call individuals like these "prophets," if we mean to use the word with its biblical sense. We do not doubt that they have seen visions and heard voices that others have neither seen nor heard. But not everyone who sees a vision or hears a voice is a prophet! These individuals, we suggest, are best understood as seers, examples of a class of especially gifted men and women known in times both ancient and modern.

Then who are the prophets for our time? We shall return to this question, after we have listened to what some of the biblical prophets have to say. But first, how ought we rightly to listen?

2

Interpreting the Prophets

The words of the prophets are not always so easy for us to understand. The Bible itself recognizes this, in the story of Philip and the Jew from Ethiopia. An official from the royal court in that country had been in Jerusalem and was on his way back to his homeland, riding in a chariot. Philip was told to intercept him on his way. As Philip jogged up alongside him, he heard the Ethiopian reading aloud from the book of the prophet Isaiah. "'Do you understand what you are reading?'" he asked. "'How can I, unless someone guides me?'" was the Ethiopian's reply. So Philip jumped up and rode along with him, helping him to understand the words of the prophetic book (Acts 8:26–40).

Our intention here is to function in the manner of Philip, sitting alongside the reader, and trying to provide a few guidelines for understanding the prophets. We suggest that when one approaches a prophetic text, two basic questions should be asked. The first is, "What *did* the text mean?" and the second, "What *does* the text mean?"

WHAT IT MEANT

The task of determining what the text meant in its own time is sometimes called "exegesis," and proceeds by asking questions of the text and then listening for answers. We can begin by asking some *historical* questions. When did the prophet live and work, and what were the conditions in his nation at that time? In order to understand the speeches of Abraham Lincoln, it is helpful to have some knowledge of nineteenth-century America and the problems that president faced. The setting for his speeches is quite different from the situation of a twentieth-century figure like John F. Kennedy. Isaiah lived in Judah in the eighth century B.C. and was very much involved in the political life of his nation. To understand his preaching, we ought to try to find out something about the hopes and fears of the people of eighth-century Judah, the burning national and international issues. And this setting will be quite different from that in which Jeremiah found himself, in the Judah of a century later. Many of these questions can be answered by studying the prophetic texts themselves with care, or by examining other biblical texts. The notes in the *Oxford Annotated Bible* or a book like John Bright's *A History of Israel* will be of great help in trying to illuminate the historical setting for a prophet.

We continue by asking some *literary* questions of the prophetic text. First, what is the extent of the unit with which we are dealing? Modern biblical scholarship has taught us that the prophetic books are actually anthologies, selections from the prophetic preaching. These selections are from sermons delivered at a variety of times and places and put into final "book" form by editors who were disciples of the prophets (note Isa. 8:16). And so if we are going to understand what the prophets said, we must begin by trying to separate these various sayings, sermons, or abridgments of sermons, from one another. As an example, note the first chapter of the book of Isaiah. Verse 1 is clearly the work of the editor who put the book together. He recognizes that it is necessary to know the historical setting for a prophet's words, and indicates that setting for us. Verses 2 and 3 form a separate unit, as do 4–9, 10–17 (notice the "Hear the word of the Lord" which signals a new beginning in 10), 18–20, 21–26 (note how "faithful city" in 21 and 26 ties this unit together), and then the chapter is rounded out with the material in 27–31.

After determining the unit, we ask about the genre or type of material with which we are dealing. Biblical scholars call this attention to genres "form criticism," and because form criticism provides us with an important key to understanding the prophets, we shall try to explain it with a few illustrations and examples.

The evening newspaper contains a number of different literary genres, including news stories, advertisements, comics, editorials, letters to the editor, political cartoons, and the like. Each of these genres has certain characteristics, and each has a particular intention. A news story is marked by attention to names, dates, and places, and intends to inform; an editorial presents an opinion on a current issue and is aimed at persuading the reader; a political cartoon may intend to amuse and to criticize. As we read through the newspaper, we make "form-critical" judgments instantly and instinctively. We do not understand a statement in a column of political satire in the same way in which we might understand the same statement in a story on the front page.

A further illustration: Let us imagine that we are watching the opening portion of the "Tonight" show on television, where Johnny Carson delivers his introductory monologue. A regular viewer of the program knows what type of material to expect in the monologue: it will be humorous, perhaps satirical, and the intention of the material will be to amuse. If the comedian should say, "In an effort to prolong the spirit of the bicentennial, the president of the United States announced today that all school buildings across the nation are to be painted red, white, and blue," we wouldn't for a moment take him literally. We might be amused, but we would not be alarmed about what would be happening to the schoolhouses down the block. However, if the same words were spoken as the leading item on the evening news broadcast, we would understand them quite differently! On the network news broadcast we expect material which is of the genre "news report," marked by careful attention to accuracy and intending to inform. The point is that identifying the genre or type of material is essential to understanding a statement correctly.

Now to some examples from the prophets. We do find historical reports in the prophetic books, material which is much like the material found on the front page or heard on a news broadcast. Isaiah 36, for example, reports the attack of Sennacherib on Jerusalem. The material is in prose form and is marked by attention to names (Hezekiah, Sennacherib), dates ("In the fourteenth year . . . "), and places. But now look at a text like Isaiah 55:12. Here the prophet is announcing that soon the people who are exiles in Babylon will be set free. The material is in poetic form and declares, "the mountains and the hills before you shall break forth into singing, and all the trees of the field shall clap their hands." Quite clearly the prophet is not making predictions about events about to take place in the natural world. He is personifying, saying that even nature will rejoice when God frees his people from captivity. This is imaginative literature and it must be read with imagination.

The prophetic books contain an amazing variety of genres. The prophet might appear in a public place in the role of a singer of ballads, putting his message in the form of an innocent-sounding song (Isa. 5:1–7). The cry of "woe" in the ancient world announced that a funeral was to take place. When the prophet pronounced a "woe" upon an individual or a group, he was announcing that there was a funeral in their future (the "woe-oracles" in Isa. 5:8–23). Much of the New Testament is made up of letters. We find a letter in the prophetic books, too, which Jeremiah sent to the exiles in Babylon (Jer. 29:4–23). The final editor of the prophetic books might insert portions of a hymn at various points, just as a modern-day preacher might quote a verse from a hymn in the course of a sermon (Amos 4:13; 5:8–9; 9:5–6; Isa. 12). The prophet may represent God and people as participants in a legal process, where God is the Accuser and the people the accused (Hos. 4:1–3; Mic. 6:1–5), or where God is Advocate for the people, taking up their cause against the leaders who crush them (Isa. 3:13–15). An especially important genre in the earlier prophets is the announcement of judgment, made up of an accusation, an announcement of punishment, and the messenger formula. Note, for example, the prophetic saying in Amos 1:3–5; here we see the messenger formula ("Thus says the LORD") followed by an accusation ("For three transgressions of Damascus, and for four, I will not revoke the punishment; because they have threshed Gilead with thresh-ing sledges of iron.") and an announcement of punishment ("So I will send a fire upon the house of Hazael . . . "). The remaining oracles in Amos 1:6—2:5 follow this same pattern; the reader can also discover the pattern in passages like Isaiah 1:21–26 or 3:16—4:1.

As we identify these various genres, we will often be able to determine where the material would have functioned in the life of ancient Israel or Judah (the "setting in life" or *Sitz im Leben*). A hymn such as we find in Isaiah 12:4–6 originally must have been a part of a worship service. The question-and-answer liturgy in Micah 6:6–8 was probably used as a worshiper was entering the temple area. The worshiper would ask the questions in 6 and 7, and the priest would give the answer found in verse 8. We could go on. But these examples are enough to indicate that the prophets were men of great creativity and imagination. If we are going to understand what they were saying, we need to read with some creativity and imagination, too.

Having settled the questions of unit and genre, we pro-ceed further by analyzing the structure of the unit. What are its natural points of division? When we are dealing with a prophetic saying which fits into the "announcement of judgment" category as described above, the structure is quite obvious. In Isaiah 1:21–26, for example, we find a complaint or accusation (21–23), a messenger formula (24a), and then an announcement of punishment (24b–26). In Isaiah 3:16—4:1 the messenger formula is at the beginning ("The LORD said") and is followed by a complaint or accusation (16) and an announcement of punishment (3:17—4:1). Most often, the reader will simply use his common sense in analyzing the structure of a prophetic unit. For instance, the sixth chapter of Isaiah presents us with the prophet's account of his call experience. It falls into the following divisions: Isaiah sees God, the Holy One (verses 1–4); Isaiah sees himself, sinful, and then forgiven (verses 5–7); Isaiah is given a task (verses 8–13).

As we continue to work at what the text meant for its own time, we move finally to consider the *message* or essential point of the text. Here it may be helpful to focus on key words in a particular saying. What did the prophet Isaiah mean by "justice" as used in 1:21? The footnotes of an annotated Bible, a concordance, a Bible dictionary, or a theological word book can all be of assistance at this point. It is often helpful to bring the message into focus by trying to summarize in a few sentences just what the text meant for its own time.

WHAT IT MEANS

But now what does the prophetic word mean for today? If we have worked carefully at determining what it meant, the contemporary relevance will usually become obvious. The ancient text begins to speak to our own time! To bring the message into focus, it may be helpful to ask two further questions: What does the text say about the relationship between God and man? What does the text say about man and his relationship to his fellow man? The interpreter should try to formulate brief answers to these questions in a manner which bridges the gap between what it meant and what it means. Taking a text like Isaiah 1:10–17 as an example, we might formulate an answer to the first question as follows: God expects of his people something more than ritual and the outward trappings of religion! And to the second question: a people which calls itself a People of God has a special responsibility toward the orphan and widow. Note that each of these statements faces two ways, describing what the text meant then, but also pointing toward what the text means now.

Of course one cannot apply the method we have described to every text in a mechanical way. But one can develop the habit of asking first what the text meant, and then what it means. And it is important to ask both questions. If we never move beyond "what it meant," our interpretation will bog down in the details of ancient history, linguistics, archaeology, or even ancient religion. But if we jump immediately to ask "what it means," without paying any attention to the message of the text for its own time, we are in danger of simply reading our own notions into the text. Certain portions of the Bible can speak quite directly to our own situation. But very often this shortcut to "what it means" is the method of the religious quack, who picks a verse here, another there, and then patches together some comments on current events and predictions of future happenings for which he claims biblical authority. Going at the task in this manner, one can use the Bible to support almost any opinion, and predict practically any event. But such is a using of the texts, rather than a listening to them.

What we are suggesting here is simply a careful listening to the prophetic text. Listening is a skill which needs to be developed. The tendency in conversation is always to be so eager to inject our own opinions that we pay little attention to what the other is actually saying. The same is the case with biblical interpretation. We need to work at asking questions of the text, and then listening to that text, expectantly and prayerfully. As we do so, we may discover that through these words from ancient times we begin to hear a Word speaking to our own time, even a Word from God.

A NOTE ON TWO RECENT BOOKS

We have already mentioned the best-sellers by Lindsey and von Däniken which offer interpretations of prophecy. Now let us look at how these books actually go about dealing with biblical texts, in the light of the comments just made.

Hal Lindsey's book, *The Late Great Planet Earth*, is described on its cover as "a penetrating look at incredible prophecies involving this generation." We might observe first of all that the author actually deals with a rather restricted selection of biblical texts. Most of his discussion concerns Daniel 7—12, Ezekiel 38—39, Zechariah 9—14, the book of Revelation, and parts of the Gospels. The reader will recognize that these are not selections from the major prophetic voices of the Bible. Lindsey does not come to grips with the essentials of the preaching of Amos, Hosea, Isaiah, Micah, Jeremiah, or the major portion of Ezekiel. Now of course it is perfectly legitimate to deal with these other parts of Scripture. But when we ask which genre these texts represent, we discover that the bulk of them belong to a special category called "apocalyptic," a type of literature which originated during times of intense persecution. Apocalyptic literature is written in a "secret code" fashion, because of the dangerous situation facing its readers, and if we are going to understand it, we have to try to get into the historical situation and crack that apocalyptic code language.

But now let us look at a couple of examples. Lindsey quotes the King James Version of Dan. 7:24:

> "And the ten horns out of this kingdom are ten kings that shall arise: and another shall rise after them; and he shall be diverse from the first, and he shall subdue three kings."[1]

We would approach this text somewhat as follows: the historical setting is the time around 167 B.C., when the Jews in Palestine were suffering a terrible persecution under the fanatic Greek ruler, Antiochus IV Epiphanes. In an effort to unify all people under his rule, Antiochus prohibited anything but the Greek religion. Thus he tried to put a stop to Jewish religious observances, including circumcision, the sabbath, and offerings. He burned copies of the Scriptures and even dedicated the temple to the Greek god Zeus. The interested reader can find the story of this persecution in 1 Maccabees 1 and 2 Maccabees 6. Out of this situation the book of Daniel comes, written partially in apocalyptic "code" and seeking to encourage its readers to hold fast to the faith. Against this background, much that appears obscure in Daniel becomes quite clear. Chapter 7, for example, describes four beasts which come out of the sea. These are identified as four kings (vs. 17). The fourth beast has ten horns (representing ten more kings, vs. 24) and a mysterious "other horn" signifying one more king who arrogantly speaks words against God and his people (7:8, 20 f., 24 f.). Those who heard these words in the second century B.C. would recognize that the fourth beast was the Greek empire under Alexander, the ten horns the kings that followed him, and the "other horn" the fanatical Antiochus IV Epiphanes. This text was saying to the suffering Jews of that time that though the power of Antiochus now seems great, God is still in control and will put an end to this boastful, blasphemous ruler! So remain loyal to the faith! And that message continues to come through to a People of God suffering persecution.

Lindsey, however, does not ask what this text might have meant in the second century. In fact, the "ten kings" are just now appearing on the stage of history. He writes, "We believe that the Common Market and the trend toward unification of Europe may well be the beginning of the ten-nation confederacy predicted by Daniel and the Book of Revelation."[2] And the boastful king has no connection with Antiochus, but is rather a mysterious "Future Fuehrer" soon to arrive on the twentieth-century scene.[3]

Another example: Seen against its background in the second century B.C., Daniel 9:27 is again referring to Antiochus:

> And he shall make a strong covenant with many for one week; and for half of the week he shall cause sacrifice and offering to cease . . .

In this chapter, a "week" means a "week of years" or seven years (vs. 24). The "covenant" was an agreement between Antiochus and those Jews who were willing to accept Greek religion. Causing sacrifices and offerings to cease for half of a week meant that Antiochus would halt worship in the temple for three and one-half years. This was in fact the case, since the temple was dedicated to Zeus in 167 B.C. and rededicated to the worship of God in 164 B.C.. Thus this text announced to the people suffering under the persecutions of Antiochus that the time of this profaning of the temple was limited!

But how does Lindsey understand this text? Again, he does not ask what it might have meant in its own time. The "strong covenant" means a pact that the "Future Fuehrer" (soon to appear in the twentieth century) will make with the Israelis, just before the return of Christ. In fact, Isaiah also spoke about this covenant, says Lindsey, calling it a "covenant with death."[4] (Isa. 28:15, 18) However, if we look at that word of Isaiah, we see that he was speaking about a covenant that had already been made, an anti-Assyrian treaty which

Judah had made with Egypt, around the year 705 B.C. To link the "strong covenant" of Daniel 9 and the "covenant of death" of Isaiah 28 with each other, and then with events yet to come in the twentieth century of our time may be imaginative, even interesting, but it certainly has nothing to do with what either the writer of Daniel or the prophet Isaiah meant!

Our criticism of Lindsey's treatment of texts from the prophets and other parts of the Bible is that he does not take Scripture seriously. He fails to listen to what the biblical word meant for its own day, before attempting to indicate what it might mean for our time. While his book may serve a purpose in reminding us that the future is in God's hands and in causing us to examine our own methods of interpretation, it is by no means a presentation of what the biblical prophets have to say about the future.

The second book is Erich von Däniken's international best-seller, *Chariots of the Gods?* which was also the basis for at least one television special, "The Search for Ancient Astronauts." The author's thesis is that our planet received visits from astronauts from some other place in the universe, thousands of years ago. These visits, he argues, explain a host of archaeological puzzles, from the gigantic statues on Easter Island, 2300 miles off the coast of Chile, to a mysterious "landing strip" in the Andes of Peru.

Of interest to us is the fact that von Däniken claims to find biblical evidence for the visits of these astronauts. He writes,

> The Old Testament gives some impressive descriptions in which God alone or his angels fly straight down from heaven making a tremendous noise and issuing clouds of smoke.[5]

Then he goes on to quote the first chapter of Ezekiel, in the King James Version:

> "And I looked, and, behold, a whirlwind came out of the north, a great cloud, and a fire infolding itself, and a brightness was about it, and out of the midst thereof as the color of amber, out

of the midst of the fire. Also out of the midst thereof came the likeness of four living creatures. And this was their appearance; they had the likeness of a man. And every one had four faces, and every one had four wings. And their feet were straight feet; and the sole of their feet was like the sole of a calf's foot: and they sparkled like the color of burnished brass."[6]

This, says von Däniken, is a description of a landing of a vehicle. Ezekiel is describing "a craft that comes from the north, emitting rays and gleaming and raising a gigantic cloud of desert sand."[7] But now let us look at the Ezekiel text in its context. Actually, nothing is said about a "craft" at all. Nor is there any hint of a landing. A cloud is mentioned, but it takes a bit of imagination to make it into a cloud of desert sand! When we ask about the genre or type of material which we have here, we discover that we are dealing with a vision report. The prophet says, "I saw visions of God." (1:1) Wind, cloud, and fire are frequently associated with such visionary descriptions in the Old Testament, as symbols of God's fearsome power (1 Kings 19:11 f., Exod. 19:16). The strange "living creatures" are also part of the typical imagery of prophetic visions (1 Kings 22:19–22, Isa. 6:1–8). The background for these mysterious winged creatures which support God's throne is apparently the fact that such "cherubim" were found as decorations, supporting royal thrones in the ancient Near East.[8]

The author continues by quoting Ezekiel 1:15–19, which speaks of the wheels with their rims full of eyes, which the prophet saw in his vision. He says, "To our present way of thinking what he saw was one of those special vehicles the Americans use in the desert and swampy terrain."[9] But again, the prophet himself is claiming to see a vision, not a reality. And in visions, as in dreams, all sorts of strange creatures and contraptions can appear. The wheels are unusual in a vision report, and apparently symbolize the mobility of the heavenly throne.

Finally, von Däniken quotes from Ezekiel 2:1: "Son of man, stand upon thy feet, and I will speak unto thee." This, he says, was the voice of the "strange apparitions" in this "craft" who wanted to talk to Ezekiel. The prophet thought they were gods, but in reality, they were astronauts landing on this planet.[10] But if we look at the biblical text, we see that the "strange apparitions" do not speak at all, and they are not identified as gods. Von Däniken omits the section in Ezekiel 1:22–28 which indicates that in the vision it was the Lord who was enthroned above these creatures; the background again is the decorative use of cherubim on actual thrones in the world of the Old Testament writer. And the voice addressing the prophet as "Son of Man" came from *above* the creatures (Ezek. 1:25) and was the voice of God himself, speaking from his heavenly throne.

Our criticism of von Däniken's handling of these prophetic texts is basically the same as our criticism of Lindsey. He simply has not done his historical and literary homework. He has made no attempt to understand what the prophetic text meant in its own sixth-century B.C. setting. In short, he has not really listened to the texts, but has used them, to support his thesis. Whether or not our planet has been visited by intelligent beings from outer space we leave as an open question. But to claim support for such a notion from Ezekiel is clearly nonsense.

3

The Powerless

On one occasion, Isaiah denounced the political leaders of his day because of their attitude and actions toward three groups of people. He pronounced a "woe" upon them, which meant that he was announcing their funeral!

> Woe to those who decree iniquitous decrees,
>   and the writers who keep writing oppression,
> to turn aside the needy from justice
>   and to rob the poor of my people of their right,
> that widows may be their spoil,
>   and that they may make the fatherless their prey!
>
> (Isa. 10:1–2)

Those responsible for enacting legislation in the Judah of Isaiah's day had put laws into effect which oppressed three groups of people: the widows, the orphans, and the poor. These three groups have in common the fact that they have no power in society and are thus easily taken advantage of. The widow has no husband to protect her, the orphan has no parents, and the poor have no money. These were—and are—representative of the powerless in any society.

The biblical prophets have a good deal to say about the powerless. But when they preach that the People of God have a special responsibility toward this group, they are saying nothing new. They are rather reminding their hearers of one of the basic features of the style of life which has always been expected of the People of God: a special kind of concern for the powerless. And before we listen to that prophetic preaching, let us note how a variety of biblical materials articulate that concern.

LAW AND COVENANT: THE THREE R'S

When the ordinary Bible reader thinks of "law" in the Old Testament, he rightly thinks first of the Ten Commandments. But chances are he remembers them from a catechism, rather than from the actual biblical text. And Luther's Catechism, for example, leaves out a very important clue to the right understanding of the Ten Commandments and, in fact, of all biblical "law."

Both versions of the Decalogue in the Bible begin in the same way:

> "I am the LORD your God, *who brought you out of the land of Egypt, out of the house of bondage.*"
>
>   (Exod. 20:2; Deut. 5:6; emphasis added)

The part in italics is omitted in Luther's Catechism. But this clause is important, because it furnishes a *reminder* of what God has done for his people. He has entered into a special *relationship* with them ("I am the LORD your God") and has delivered them from slavery in Egypt. After the reminder the commandments spell out the expected *response* of God's people. They describe the kind of reaction expected to God's prior action. These three r's—reminder, relationship, response—are essential for a proper understanding of law in the Bible.

The larger context of the Decalogue makes the same point. First there is the reminder of God's act of deliverance, the Exodus (Exod. 1—15). Then the special relationship is formalized in the agreement or covenant which God makes with his people (Exod. 19—24). Finally, the expected response of the people is spelled out in the large block of mainly "commandment" material associated with the Mt. Sinai events, running all the way through the remainder of the book of Exodus, Leviticus, and through Numbers 10:10.

This puts a new light on the commandments. They do not define a legal relationship, in the manner of a contract, but rather indicate the kind of grateful response expected from a people who have already experienced God's delivering and sustaining love. To illustrate: a relationship between an employer and an employee is a legal kind of relationship. If I am working for someone, I will do certain things for him. I will put in an honest eight hours each day (with coffee breaks), and will try to do quality work. I may even put in some time evenings and weekends, if given the chance. But why do I do these things for my employer? Because I love him? No. Rather, because I know that the more I do for him, the more he'll do for me. And there is a contract which defines our relationship, in terms of so many dollars per hour. But the God/people relationship is not of this kind at all! The covenant is different from a contract. This relationship is more like that between a parent and a child. Through the years, the parent has done much for the child, caring for him, providing food and clothing, making his life possible. Then perhaps one day the child decides that he wants to do something for his parents. He too may work hard, put in some time evenings, weekends, or whatever. But his motivation is quite different from that of the employee. His work is a grateful response to the good things that his parents have done for him. The first relationship is a legal one, the second based on love.

That reminder of what God has done for his people as expressed in Exodus 20:2 marks the God/people relationship as one of the second type, initiated and maintained by love. The commandments which follow sketch the kind of response expected of God's people. That response will mean a life-style marked by a certain attitude toward God (Exod. 20:3–11) and a certain attitude toward people (Exod. 20:12–17). Jesus summarized these two dimensions of the expected response of the People of God even more simply when he said:

> "You shall love the Lord your God with all your heart, and with all your soul, and with all your mind. This is the great and first commandment. And a second is like it, You shall love your neighbor as yourself." (Matt. 22:37–39)

But the love commandment which Jesus gave does not really provide specific directions for living the kind of life expected of the people of God. And, in fact, the Ten Commandments are also only very general guidelines, most often indicating what God's people ought *not* to do. There are other materials which give more explicit directives. These too should be understood as defining the expected response of a people who have a certain relationship to their God. Our concern here will be with three such collections of legal materials, and with what they have to say about the powerless.

LAW AND THE POWERLESS

After the Ten Commandments in Exodus 20, we find a collection of laws called the Book of the Covenant (Exod. 20:22—23:33). This material comes from the earliest period in the history of Israel, the time after the conquest and before the monarchy, when the people were ruled by "judges" (about 1240–1020 B.C.). This early law collection exhibits a good deal of concern for the powerless:

> "You shall not wrong a stranger or oppress him, for you were strangers in the land of Egypt. You shall not afflict any widow or orphan. If you do afflict them, and they cry out to me, I will surely hear their cry; and my wrath will burn, and I will kill you with the sword, and your wives shall become widows and your children fatherless." (Exod. 22:21–24)

Notice that the commandment about the stranger is supported by a *reminder* of the Exodus event. The sense is, "Remember, you were strangers, and God delivered you; therefore respond by showing concern to the stranger among you!" The commandment concerning the widow and the orphan is supported by the statement that God himself is watching over their rights; we shall discover this same notion later, when we hear the prophet Isaiah describe the Lord as Advocate for the powerless (Isa. 3:13–15). The stranger is again mentioned in Exodus 23:9. Other laws in this collection prohibit excessive interest rates charged to the poor (22:25) and make provisions for the poor to gather from the fields every seventh year (23:10–11). A special concern is that the poor man get fair treatment in the courts (23:6), but not that he be shown favoritism just because he is poor (23:3).

The book of Deuteronomy (meaning "second law") takes its name from the fact that the giving of the commandments on Mount Sinai is reported a second time (Deut. 5). The book itself is a summary of sermons preached at worship services where the covenant was renewed and the people rededicated themselves to their calling as the People of God. The heart of the book contains preaching which takes up ancient legal materials and applies them to the present situation of the hearers. Thus while the final form of the book is probably from the seventh century B.C., like all preaching it is based upon older texts and seeks to apply these texts to a new situation in a fresh way. As Deuteronomy picks up the kind of commandments that we have already noted in the Book of the Covenant, it becomes especially clear that what the people are to do is considered as the expected response to what God has already done. Chapters 1–3 set the tone for what follows with a reminder of how God guided his people in the wilderness. Note how the reminder/response structure is evident in Deut. 4:37–40:

> "And because he loved your fathers and chose their descendants after them, and brought you out of Egypt with his own presence, by his great power, driving out before you nations

greater and mightier than yourselves, to bring you in, to give
you their land for an inheritance, as at this day; know therefore
this day, and lay it to your heart, that the LORD is God in
heaven above and on the earth beneath; there is no other
[*reminder*]. Therefore you shall keep his statutes and his commandments, which I command you this day . . . "[expected
response].

The same structure is very clear in a passage like 7:6–11
(reminder of what God has done, 6–10; expected response,11). This expected response of the people of God as
spelled out in these sermons in Deuteronomy again shows
special concern for the powerless. The tithe is for their support (14:28–29;26:12–15), and the people are to be generous in
caring for them (15:7–11). The widow, orphan, and sojourner
are to take part in the festival celebrations (16:9–15). Em-
ployers are advised to pay employees immediately, and not
oppress them; God watches over them (24:14–15). Their legal
rights are to be guarded (24:17–18). And, in a rather unique
welfare distribution system, the widow, orphan, and
sojourner were to be allowed to have the remains of the
harvest (24:19–22; cf. Ruth 2).

There is yet another block of legal material which is
related to our theme. This is the "Holiness Code" found in
Leviticus 17—26, and called by that name because of the
frequently repeated statement, "'You shall be holy, for I the
Lord your God am holy.'" (Lev. 19:2; 20:7, etc.) "Holy" here
has the sense of "separate," and the laws in this collection are
designed to help the people of God maintain a life-style
properly separate from the world in which they find themselves. Though the materials themselves are doubtless quite
ancient, the collection appears to have taken shape after
Deuteronomy, in the sixth century B.C.. Once again, these
commandments are to be understood as the expected response of a people reminded of their special covenant relationship to God (18:1–5; 20:26; 22:31–33). We find the

command to leave something after the harvest for the poor and sojourner (19:9–10), to give impartial judgment in the courts (19:15), to protect the stranger (19:33 f.), and generally to care for the poverty stricken (25:35–38). Another class of the powerless is named: the aged, with the command, "You shall rise in the presence of grey hairs, give honour to the aged, and fear your God." (Lev. 19:32, N.E.B.)

To summarize our investigation of these legal materials: law or commandment in these collections should always be understood in the context of the covenant between God and people. The people are reminded of what God has done for them, enjoy a special relationship to him, and are then expected to respond in a certain way. An important part of that response throughout all of these collections is a special concern for the powerless, including the widow, the orphan, the poor, the stranger, and even the aged.

PROVERBS AND THE POWERLESS

We don't know much about education in ancient Israel. It is reasonable to assume that much of it took place in the family or the extended family, just as it does today. But there are hints that there were schools as well. David, for example, is first introduced to us as a young boy who takes care of his father's sheep (1 Sam. 16:11). But when he is a candidate for service at the court of King Saul, one of the servants describes him as "skilful in playing, a man of valor, a man of war, prudent in speech, and a man of good presence." (1 Sam. 16:18) We would call him cultured and well-educated, and he must have received his education in some sort of school in the little town of Bethlehem from which he came. We can be certain that there were schools connected with the royal court in Jerusalem, just as there were in the courts of Egypt and Mesopotamia.

The Book of Proverbs is a collection of short essays and sayings used for instruction in the court at Jerusalem. While much of the material was collected and composed during the time of Solomon in the tenth century (Prov. 1:1; 10:1) and re-edited and supplemented during the time of Hezekiah in the eighth century (25:1), its origins are even more ancient and amazingly diverse. No doubt a good part of the material grew out of the education that took place in the family and extended family. But some came from outside of Israel. The section in 22:17—24:22 contains a good deal of material borrowed from the courts of Egypt, and re-shaped to fit the needs of Israel.[1] While the text is not certain, "The words of Agur son of Jakeh of Massa" (30:1) and "The words of Lemuel, king of Massa . . . " (31:1) apparently identify materials which originated in north Arabia (cf. Gen. 25:14). Israel was very much open to the best instructional materials from the nations around her!

The various forms found in Proverbs give some clues as to how the materials might have been used in the classroom. Chapter 10:1 ff. provides a series of examples of antithetic parallelism. We might imagine the teacher giving the first half of the saying, and the pupil responding with the second half:

(Teacher) A wise son makes a glad father,
(Pupil)   but a foolish son is a sorrow to his mother. (10:1)
(Teacher) A slack hand causes poverty,
(Pupil)   but the hand of the diligent makes rich. (10:4)

Or the teacher might ask the riddle, "Who has woe? Who has sorrow? Who has strife? Who has complaining? Who has wounds without cause? Who has redness of eyes?" (23:29) The pupil would respond, "Those who tarry long over wine, those who go to try mixed wine." (23:30) Then the teacher would continue with some practical advice about the use of alcohol:

Do not look at wine when it is red,
    when it sparkles in the cup
    and goes down smoothly.
At the last it bites like a serpent,

and stings like an adder.
Your eyes will see strange things,
and your mind utter perverse things. (23:31–33)

The series of numerical sayings in 30:15 ff. can also be understood in a schoolroom setting. The teacher might ask, "Name three or four things that inspire wonder." The pupil would answer:

the way of an eagle in the sky,
the way of a serpent on a rock,
the way of a ship on the high seas,
and the way of a man with a maiden. (30:19)

Or the teacher would say, "Name four things which are small, but exceedingly wise." The pupil would answer:

the ants are a people not strong,
yet they provide their food in the summer;
the badgers are a people not mighty,
yet they make their homes in the rocks;
the locusts have no king,
yet all of them march in rank;
the lizard you can take in your hands,
yet it is in kings' palaces. (30:25–28)

But what does this material in Proverbs have to do with our theme? In the first place, the prophets Amos and Isaiah appear to have been greatly influenced by just the kind of "wisdom" materials that we find in Proverbs. Their own education, whether in family or in school, must have included a thorough grounding in proverbial wisdom. Secondly, a special concern of this wisdom material is the care of the powerless—the widow, the orphan, and particularly the poor.

The reader can discover these references for himself. One ought to be alert to the cry of the poor, because

He who closes his ear to the cry of the poor
will himself cry out and not be heard. (21:13)

Those who have ought to share with the poor who have not,

> He who has a bountiful eye will be blessed,
>> for he shares his bread with the poor. (22:9)

The Israelite is also called to watch over the legal rights of the poor,

> A righteous man knows the rights of the poor;
>> a wicked man does not understand such knowledge. (29:7)

The one who is concerned about the poor will find happiness,

> He who despises his neighbor is a sinner,
>> but happy is he who is kind to the poor. (14:21)

In fact, one's attitude toward the poor is an indication of his attitude toward God,

> He who oppresses a poor man insults his Maker,
>> but he who is kind to the needy honors him. (14:31)
> He who is kind to the poor lends to the LORD,
>> and he will repay him for his deed. (19:17)

The description of the ideal wife includes among her virtues a concern for the poor,

> She opens her hand to the poor,
>> and reaches out her hands to the needy. (31:20)

Watching over the rights of the poor was a special obligation of the king,

> If a king judges the poor with equity
>> his throne will be established for ever. (29:14)
> Open your mouth, judge righteously,
>> maintain the rights of the poor and needy. (31:9)

Two imperatives directed toward young men in Israel who would one day assume positions of leadership advise them to watch over the rights of the poor and the orphan. If they fail to do so, God himself will take up the cause of the poor against their oppressors!

> Do not rob the poor, because he is poor,
>   or crush the afflicted at the gate;
> for the LORD will plead their cause
>   and despoil of life those who despoil them. (22:22–23)
> Do not remove an ancient landmark
>   or enter the fields of the fatherless;
> for their Redeemer is strong;
>   he will plead their cause against you. (23:10–11)[2]

God even watches over the boundary markers at the edges of the widow's land,

> The LORD tears down the house of the proud,
>   but maintains the widow's boundaries. (15:25)

THE PEOPLE OF GOD AND THE POWERLESS

We have seen that a special concern for the powerless runs through both legal and educational materials from ancient Israel. We could continue our investigation of this theme in the Old Testament by noting a number of psalms which are prayers of the poor (Ps. 40:17: 74:19: 86:1; 109:22, etc.); in our next chapter we shall look at a psalm which spells out the king's obligations toward the powerless. But the point has been made that care for the widow, orphan, and poor is central to what is expected in the life-style of a people which calls itself a People of God.

This same concern is also found in the New Testament. In Matthew 25:31 ff., Jesus is describing the great judgment scene at the end of all history. At this time, in words which are a dramatic development of Proverbs 14:31 and 19:17, Christ the King will declare to his people that when they cared for the hungry, the thirsty, the stranger, the naked, the sick, and the prisoner, they actually encountered him in the midst of the world! When they ask, "Lord, when did we see thee hungry and feed thee, or thirsty and give thee drink?" he will answer, "As you did it to one of the least of these my brethren, you did it to me." We might also call attention to a definition of religion which the New Testament offers. Surprisingly, nothing is said about creeds, sacrifices, worship, or prayer: "Religion that is pure and undefiled before God and the Father is this: to visit orphans and widows in their affliction, and to keep oneself unstained from the world." (James 1:27) Thus religion becomes a very practical matter, defined in terms of a relationship to the powerless. It just won't do to say to the one who is cold and hungry, "Go in peace!" He doesn't need words, but food and clothing! (James 2:14 ff.)

The New Testament imperatives which call Christians to a certain way of living should also be understood in terms of the "three R's" which helped us to understand the Old Testament commandments. Christians are those who have heard and believed the Good News about what God has done through Jesus Christ, in fulfillment of the promises of the Old Testament (the sermons in Acts 1—10, the Gospels). They are continually *reminded* of this Good News which is at the foundation of their new life (1 Cor. 15:1–11, as an example). And they enjoy a special *relationship* to God, as people with whom a New Covenant has been made (1 Cor. 11:23–26). They are, in fact " . . . a chosen race, a royal priesthood, a holy nation, God's own people . . . ." (1 Peter 2:9) Finally, this new People of God is expected to *respond* to what God has done with love to God and to the neighbor (Matt. 22:37–39). The fact that love is the expected response to what God has done is particularly evident in the first letter of John: "Beloved, if God so loved us, we also ought to love one another." (1 John 4:11) "We love, because he first loved us." (1 John 4:19)

In sum, as we look at the story of the People of God from the time of the Judges to the time of James, from a thousand years before Christ through the first century after, one theme keeps sounding through. A people which calls itself a People of God has always been charged with a special responsibility toward the widow, the orphan, the poor, the stranger—the powerless. But as we hear this, we may become a bit restless. And it may be well, though not necessarily comforting, to remind ourselves who we really are, if we call ourselves Christian. I recall one of the first actions of a friend when he took charge of a little church in the community of Drewry's Bluff, Virginia. The sign in front of the church said, "Drewry's Bluff Presbyterian Church." But in the space below he added, "Assembles Here." That helped to remind those people that Drewry's Bluff Presbyterian Church was really not a building, but a people, in fact a People of God who assembled there briefly each week, and who then went back out into the world to be about their business as God's men, women, and children.

If we call ourselves Christians, we are part of that new People of God described in the New Testament. We reaffirm the covenant relationship with our God when we celebrate the Lord's Supper and hear those words, "This cup is the new covenant in my blood." We are reminded week by week of what God has done for us in Christ, through sermon, song, and liturgy: "Almighty God, our Heavenly Father, has had mercy upon us, and has given his only begotten Son to die for us, and for his sake forgives us all our sins." But then, we ask, how ought we to respond? We conclude with a story which William Stringfellow has told:

> . . . I had one day to fly to Boston to visit the Harvard Business School to give a lecture. I was late . . . in leaving my apartment to get out to the airport. Just as I was about to go, the telephone rang. I had not the will power not to answer it, in spite of my rush. It was a clergyman who was calling. "I have a woman in my office," he told me, "who is going to be evicted in the morning. Tell me what to do for her." I asked him a few questions and, as it turned out, the grounds for the eviction were the non-payment of the rent. The woman apparently had no money to pay her rent. She had, or asserted that she had, certain complaints against the landlord, but the complaints that

she had were not sufficient, assuming that they could be legally established, to justify non-payment of the rent. They were no defense to the eviction, and if she wished to pursue them it would have to be done in a separate action against the landlord, apart from the eviction proceeding. By this time I was even more anxious about catching the airplane and said to the minister, "Well, sell one of your tapestries and pay the rent," and hung up and caught the plane. On the plane I thought the telephone conversation over and thought that perhaps I had been rude and too abrupt in answering the minister that way and I considered calling him back after landing to apologize. But by the time the plane landed at Logan Airport I had rejected that idea. My answer had not been rude or irresponsible. On the contrary, exactly what he and the people of his congregation, which does have several beautiful and valuable tapestries, must be free to do is to sell their tapestries to pay the rent—to pay somebody else's rent—to pay anybody's rent who can't pay their own rent . . . The tapestry hanging in a church becomes and is a wholesome and holy thing, an appropriate and decent part of the scene of worship, only if the congregation which has the tapestry is free to take it down and sell it in order to feed the hungry or care for the sick or pay the rent or in any other way serve the world.[3]

The Church is people, the People of God. And the People of God are called to care for the powerless.

4

The Arrogance of Power

We have seen something of the responsibilities of the whole People of God toward the powerless as we have looked at legal and wisdom materials from the Old Testament and glanced at Gospel and Letter in the New Testament. But now what about the particular responsibilities of those who exercise political power?

For over 400 years monarchy was the form of government in Israel, then in Israel and Judah. Saul, David, and Solomon presided over a united kingdom for a century, beginning in 1020 B.C. After Solomon's death in 922 B.C., the kingdom split, with the northern part retaining the name Israel and the southerners taking the name Judah. This period of divided kingdom lasted just two hundred years, until Israel fell to the Assyrian armies in 722 B.C. From then on Judah remained alone, until the Babylonians captured the capital city of Jerusalem in 587 B.C., bringing the time of the monarchy to an end.

A monarchical form of government has certain advantages, among them efficiency and the potential for a certain smoothness of operation. But there is one great disadvantage. The ruler may become arrogant, intoxicated with power, and then set himself above the kind of morality expected of ordinary men. Among Israel's neighbors, particularly in Egypt and Mesopotamia, the ruler could be exalted to a superhuman or even semi-divine position. This tendency toward arrogance was apparent in Israel and Judah, too. The stories about the kings in 1 and 2 Samuel, 1 and 2 Kings, and 1 and 2 Chronicles provide plenty of illustrations of Lord Acton's famous statement that power tends to corrupt, and absolute power corrupts absolutely.

The monarchy was instituted in Israel in response to the request of the elders, " . . . now appoint for us a king to govern us like all the nations." (1 Sam. 8:5) And while the trappings of kingship did make her "like the other nations," there was something unique about the monarchy in Israel. The time of the kings was also the time of the great prophets. The first of the kings, Saul, was installed by the first prophet, Samuel (1 Sam. 10). Then the succession of kings and prophets run alongside one another, with the prophet firing his "Thus says the Lord" into the affairs of his nation at crucial points, as a reminder that the ultimate authority over this people was God. The last king, Zedekiah, was taken to live in Babylonian exile with his people after the fall of Jerusalem in 587 B.C. There were prophets who interpreted this tragic event and who announced a better day coming (Ezekiel, Isaiah 40—66). But after them, prophecy begins to fade away and eventually blends into apocalyptic, as exemplified by the kind of material found in the last half of the book of Daniel.

The time of the prophets was the time of the kings. And the earliest of the prophets did not deliver their oracles to the nation as a whole, but to the king as an individual. When the monarch became arrogant and began oppressing the powerless, a messenger from God would appear on the scene with his "Thus says the Lord" to remind him of the obligations that went with power.

THE OBLIGATIONS OF POWER

The king in ancient Israel and Judah was not above the laws which applied to other men. He, too, was subject to the Ten Commandments and the kind of covenant law that we have examined in the previous chapter. This is made explicitly clear in a passage from Deuteronomy which speaks about the king:

> "And when he sits on the throne of his kingdom, he shall write for himself in a book a copy of this law, from that which is in charge of the Levitical priests; and it shall be with him, and he shall read in it all the days of his life, that he may learn to fear the LORD his God, by keeping all the words of this law and these statutes, and doing them; *that his heart may not be lifted up above his brethren*, and that he may not turn aside from the commandment, either to the right hand or to the left; so that he may continue long in his kingdom, he and his children, in Israel." (Deut. 17:18–20, emphasis added)

Not only was the king subject to the law, but he was also obligated to see that it was properly administered. In other words, he was expected to maintain justice in his nation. This obligation is spelled out in Psalm 72, which must have been used as part of a royal inauguration and probably also at ceremonies observing the anniversary of an inauguration. The psalm is really a prayer on behalf of the king and his administration, and shows particular concern for his attitude toward the powerless:

> Give the king thy justice, O God,
>> and thy righteousness to the royal son!
> May he judge thy people with righteousness,
>> and thy poor with justice! (1 f.)
> May he defend the cause of the poor of the people,
>> give deliverance to the needy,
>> and crush the oppressor! (4)

Then the king's rule is described in ideal terms:

> For he delivers the needy when he calls,
>> the poor and him who has no helper.
> He has pity on the weak and the needy,
>> and saves the lives of the needy.
> From oppression and violence he redeems their life;
>> and precious is their blood in his sight. (12–14)

We have already mentioned the educational function of the material which now makes up our book of Proverbs. We said that while much of it originated in the life of the family and clan and served there to give direction for each new generation, this wisdom material also had a special use in the royal court in Jerusalem. There it educated those who would one day assume positions of leadership in the nation. We might assume that the king who heard Psalm 72 as his inaugural prayer had earlier sat in the Jerusalem schools where he had been taught that,

> If a king judges the poor with equity
>> his throne will be established for ever. (Prov. 29:14)

And also,

> Like a roaring lion or a charging bear
>> is a wicked ruler over a poor people. (Prov. 28:15)

Israel had established the monarchy in imitation of neighboring nations, and she also borrowed educational materials from her neighbors. Proverbs 31:1–9 is identified as instruction for royalty taken over from Massa, in northwest Arabia (vs. 1). The king is advised of his special responsibility for the powerless:

> Open your mouth for the dumb,
>> for the rights of all who are left desolate.
> Open your mouth, judge righteously,
>> maintain the rights of the poor and needy.
>>>> (Prov. 31:8 f.)

A number of texts from ancient Egypt, called "Instructions," provide direction for future leadership and were used in the Egyptian schools connected with the royal court.[1] The block of material in Proverbs 22:17—24:22 contains such striking parallels in both form and content to one of these works, the "Instruction of Amen-em-ope," that we may assume that the Israelite wisdom teachers appropriated and adapted the Egyptian material for their own use. This segment of Proverbs is identified as "thirty sayings"; (22:20) the Egyptian work has thirty chapters. And practically every one of the first ten sayings (22:22—23:11) has a parallel in Amen-em-ope. These sayings are obviously directed at future leadership; they are the ones who will one day "sit down to eat with a ruler" (23:1) and who should know how to conduct themselves properly at table. But now we call attention to the first and the last of these ten directives for future leaders:

> Do not rob the poor, because he is poor,
>   or crush the afflicted at the gate;
> for the LORD will plead their cause
>   and despoil of life those who despoil them.
>   (Prov. 22:22–23)

> Do not remove an ancient landmark
>   or enter the fields of the fatherless;
> for their Redeemer is strong;
>   he will plead their cause against you.
>   (Prov. 23:10–11)

The first and last of these instructions for future politicians have to do with the obligations of power toward the powerless. And the seriousness of these directives is underlined with the announcement that if the leaders do oppress the powerless, their case will come up in God's "Supreme Court," and the Lord himself will argue the cause of the poor against their oppressors! Remember these words from Proverbs. We shall hear the prophet Isaiah pick them up, when he accuses the politicians of his day of failing in their obligations, and tells them that the case of the people vs. the political leadership has come up in the heavenly courtroom, with God himself taking up the cause of the people (Isa. 3:13–15)!

Thus law, psalm, and wisdom material served to define the obligations of power in ancient Israel. But what happened when a king forgot those obligations?

DAVID AND NATHAN

The Israelis today still sing a song about King David,

David, melek Yisrael, chai, chai, v'kayam.
(David, King of Israel, live, live forever!)

A thousand years after David, Paul preached a sermon in which he remembered him as the one about whom God said, " 'I have found in David the son of Jesse a man after my heart, who will do all my will.' " (Acts 13:22) He was the greatest of the kings of Israel. The youngest of Jesse's sons, from the insignificant little town of Bethlehem, he rose from shepherd boy to king (1 Sam. 16). He was just what his country needed. A warrior who could put Israel on the map internationally. A political genius who captured a Canaanite city on neutral ground and made it the nation's capital (2 Sam. 5:6–10). A cultured man, who was an accomplished musician and a gifted public speaker (1 Sam. 16:18). And, most important, David was a man of God, who showed his serious concern for the historic faith of his people by bringing the Ark of the Covenant, the portable shrine which had accompanied Israel in her wilderness wanderings, to Jerusalem, making that city the religious as well as the political capital of the nation (2 Sam. 6).

But David was a man, not a god, and the Bible tells of his failings as well as his glories. There was the incident with Bathsheba, related in 2 Sam. 11 and 12. It was springtime in Jerusalem, the time "when kings go forth to battle." But on this occasion David stayed in Jerusalem, leaving the campaigning against the Ammonites to his trusted general, Joab. After his mid-day nap, the king walked out on the flat roof, in the cool of the late afternoon. (The routine is still the same in Jerusalem today . . . a nap in the heat of mid-day, and then perhaps a cool drink on the roof-patio.) Then David saw a beautiful woman bathing on another roof, and he wanted her. And he, you see, was king, with a good deal of power. So he inquired about the woman and found out that she was Bathsheba, the wife of a man named Uriah, a foreigner who was out in the field with the Israelite army. The situation seemed just right: the husband away, the beautiful wife home alone and no doubt a bit lonely. So David summoned her to the royal palace, made love to her, and sent her home.

A rather innocent affair, it seemed, which did no one any harm. But then one day one of the palace aides delivered a note to the king. It was from Bathsheba, and said simply, "I am pregnant." Now what should he do?

The biblical writer shows us how the man of power now moves into action, first sending off a communique to general Joab, at the front. "Send me Uriah the Hittite," the order reads. No questions are asked, and with military efficiency Uriah appears before the king, no doubt a bit mystified. David makes some small talk with him. "How is Joab doing? How is the morale among the men? How does the war look, from the viewpoint of the common infantryman?" Perhaps he said, "This is part of an effort to give selected soldiers a bit of a furlough, to indicate how much their country appreciates them." Then after this no doubt pleasant exchange, the king suggested casually, "Go down to your house, and wash your feet," which meant, "Now go home Uriah, take a few days off, and be with your good wife." The king even sent a present ahead of the soldier, perhaps an expensive wine from the royal wine cellar, so that he and his wife could enjoy these days together. (And so that Bathsheba's pregnancy would be explained!)

An ingenious plan, and we may imagine the king congratulating himself as Uriah left the palace. But Uriah? He " . . . slept at the door of the king's house with all the servants of his lord, and did not go down to his house." (2 Sam. 11:9) When David heard this, he became a bit nervous. His carefully engineered plot to explain Bathsheba's pregnancy in a perfectly logical manner was faltering. Perhaps he sensed a national scandal. But what was the matter with this Uriah fellow? The king went out to talk with him. "Haven't you come from a long journey? Why not go home, man?" But apparently this foreigner is one of those military fanatics, the "good soldier" type. He says, "All the soldiers of Israel and Judah and my general, Joab, are camping out in the open field. Should I then go home to eat and drink and sleep with my wife? I wouldn't think of it!" Then David tries again. He invites the man to a dinner with the king. Who would have dreamt of such an honor? And the king gets him drunk. "Now, Uriah, go home," says David as he ushers him out of the palace. But Uriah chooses again to sleep in the open, on an army blanket with the servants.

Now the plot begins to thicken, and we see how David, the man of power, continues to wield that power. He gives Uriah, who must have been puzzled by all this attention, a note to give to General Joab. David knows that this straight-arrow type will never break the seal and read it! It is his own death warrant! The message reads, "Put Uriah in the front lines where the fighting is hardest, and then draw back so that he is killed." Again Joab obeys without question, and efficiently carries out the orders.

Then we see David getting the report from the front. The messenger tells him how the battle has been going, and ends by mentioning that Uriah the Hittite is on the casualty list. The king, we might imagine, breathes a sigh of relief. And then he sends a message back to Joab, " 'Do not let this matter trouble you, for the sword devours now one, and now another . . . .' " (2 Sam. 11:25) That's the way it goes in wartime! Then Bathsheba gets the official message: "We regret to inform you . . . ." She mourns the death of her husband. After waiting a proper length of time, David brings her to the palace and she becomes his wife.

And so it would appear that finally the whole tawdry affair is over. Uriah has died for his country. His wife is one of many honored war widows. And the king? What has he done? " 'Why it is nothing less than a most noble, magnanimous, kingly act—an act to inspire the whole military profession— that the king marries the widow of a warrior who fell for the fatherland!' " [2] What began as adultery and then moved into murder has come to rest. But for the narrator's note in the biblical account, "But the thing that David had done displeased the LORD." (2 Sam. 11:27)

Now the prophet Nathan enters. He is a respected man, known to David, no doubt a frequent visitor in the royal quarters. This day he begins, "Your majesty, let me tell you about something which has just happened." And he goes on as follows,

> "There were two men in a certain city, the one rich and the other poor. The rich man had very many flocks and herds; but the poor man had nothing but one little ewe lamb, which he had bought. And he brought it up, and it grew up with him and with his children; it used to eat of his morsel, and drink from his cup, and lie in his bosom, and it was like a daughter to him. Now there came a traveler to the rich man, and he was unwilling to take one of his own flock or herd to prepare for the wayfarer who had come to him, but he took the poor man's lamb, and prepared it for the man who had come to him." (2 Sam. 12:1–4)

The king reacts instantly, coming to the defense of the poor man, as a king should. " 'As the LORD lives, the man who has done this deserves to die . . . .' " (2 Sam. 12:5) Then Nathan wheels on the king and says, "You're the man!" He delivers a message from God, first reminding David what God had done for him:

> "Thus says the LORD, the God of Israel, 'I anointed you king over Israel, and I delivered you out of the hand of Saul; and I gave you your master's house, and your master's wives into

> your bosom, and gave you the house of Israel and of Judah; and if this were too little, I would add to you as much more.'" (2 Sam. 12:7–8)

Then he continues by pointing out how David had responded,

> "Why have you despised the word of the LORD, to do what is evil in his sight? You have smitten Uriah the Hittite with the sword, and have taken his wife to be your wife, and have slain him with the sword of the Ammonites." (2 Sam. 12:9)

After this accusation Nathan announces the doom that will come upon David,

> "Now therefore the sword shall never depart from your house . . . ." (2 Sam. 12:10)

And the narrative continues to show how a shadow falls over the house of David from this point on. When the arrogance of power resulted in the oppression and even destruction of the powerless, the prophet intervened with a word from God. But let us look at yet another incident.

ELIJAH AND AHAB

If David is remembered as the greatest king to rule over Israel, the biblical writers recall Ahab as one of the worst. The historian who gave us the account in Kings summarizes his administration in this way:

> And Ahab the son of Omri did evil in the sight of the LORD more than all that were before him. (1 Kings 16:30)

Much had happened since the days of King David. In 922 B.C., after the death of Solomon, the northern tribes seceded from the kingdom, retaining the name Israel and leaving Judah with its capital Jerusalem in the south. It was over this northern kingdom of Israel that Ahab ruled, from 869–850 B.C.

The previous incident began when a king coveted another man's wife, and showed how he exercised his power to use and to destroy persons. This incident begins with a king coveting another man's property. We can imagine the situation, as it is described in 1 Kings 21. A man named Naboth had a vineyard in the beautiful Jezreel valley. Today the traveler can drive his automobile to the site of ancient Megiddo, walk up to see the remains of the stables that Ahab had built there, and look down upon the green valley. As one reads the account in 1 Kings, it may strike him that things have not really changed so much. I recall a real estate agent telling us that the three most important things to remember about buying property are first, location; second, location; and third, location! And this was precisely the issue with Naboth's vineyard. It was located near Ahab's house and the king, with a bit of farmer's blood in him, wanted it for a vegetable garden. "I'll give you a better piece of land in exchange for it," he said, "or I'll pay you, whichever you'd rather."

But Naboth wouldn't sell. The land had been in his family for generations. He had inherited it. And there were even religious reasons for holding on to it. Israelite law was quite clear on the point. The Lord said,

> The land shall not be sold in perpetuity, for the land is mine; for you are strangers and sojourners with me. (Lev. 25:23)

Ancient laws like this prevented the rich from buying up all of the land from the poor, and the king knew that he was subject to these laws, too (cf. also Lev. 25:10, 13–17, 34). Then we have an intimate picture of the king in his private quarters, lying on his bed, sulking like a child, and refusing to eat (1 Kings 21:4).

Ahab's wife Jezebel enters. "Why aren't you eating?" she asks. "Because Naboth won't give me his vineyard," Ahab answers, "neither for money, nor for another piece of property." And Jezebel, who remains an example of everything a Hebrew woman ought not to be, asks "What kind of king are you?" and takes matters into her own hands. She arranges a community gathering, where Naboth would be present. She finds two hoodlums who will falsely accuse him of both religious blasphemy and national treason. On the strength of the testimony of two (cf. Deut. 19:15) Naboth is found guilty, taken outside the city, and stoned to death. Jezebel the queen has a good deal of power, and she knows how to use it! She returns to Ahab and tells him, " 'Arise, take possession of the vineyard of Naboth the Jezreelite, which he refused to give you for money; for Naboth is not alive, but dead.' " (1 Kings 21:15) And the matter was done with.

But not really. The narrative continues, "Then the word of the LORD came to Elijah the Tishbite, saying, 'Arise, go down to meet Ahab, king of Israel, who is in Samaria; behold, he is in the vineyard of Naboth, where he has gone to take possession.' " (1 Kings 21:17–18) The crusty prophet finds the king inspecting his new garden plot and trying to decide, we might assume, where to put the carrots, the tomatoes, and the peas. Ahab looks up and says, " 'Have you found me, O my enemy?' " " 'I have found you,' " answers Elijah, and then he delivers a message from the Lord:

> "Thus says the LORD, 'Have you killed and also taken possession? . . . In the place where dogs licked up the blood of Naboth shall dogs lick your own blood.' " (1 Kings 21:19)

The prophet delivers another oracle against Jezebel, and the account ends with the king as dejected as he was at the beginning. Finally, Ahab is killed in battle, and the narrator adds a grim concluding note:

> So the king died, and was brought to Samaria; and they buried the king in Samaria. And they washed the chariot by the pool of Samaria, and the dogs licked up his blood. . . . (1 Kings 22:37 f.)

Once again the arrogant exercise of power had resulted in the crushing of the powerless, and had called forth an announcement of punishment from God's prophet.

THE ARROGANCE OF POWER

What shall we do with these stories of prophets and kings, with their antique and even gruesome flavor? In our sophistication we might find them a bit embarrassing and recommend that we eliminate them from our teaching and preaching, perhaps judging the material as not suited for young, or at least proper audiences! We may wish that we hadn't even heard about the sordid affair between David and Bathsheba! In fact, a later biblical historian took precisely this approach. The writer of 1 Chronicles uses 2 Samuel as a source. But notice how 1 Chronicles 20 begins by quoting 2 Samuel 11:1, and then continues by cutting out the whole Bathsheba incident, from 2 Samuel 11:2—12:25! And surely the bloody business about Ahab and Naboth is not in taste for modern times! But this option is really not open to us, if we consider ourselves to be a part of that People of God for whom the Bible is the source and norm for all matters of faith and life.

If we are not so bold as to eliminate these stories, perhaps we can appreciate them, in the manner of a course in "Bible as Literature." We might call attention to a subtle nuance here, the touch of a redactor there, delight over an allusion, or puzzle at a geographical discrepancy. But somehow this doesn't quite do it, either. We start out as detached critics making judgments about the stories. Then, like David listening to Nathan, we get involved in the story and our anger becomes kindled at that person who took advantage of the powerless. And suddenly we find the story involving us, the words judging us, and we are faced with that prophetic accusation, "You are the man!"

And so there is a third possibility. It seems the more we listen to these stories, the more they demand that we appropriate them to our own situation, if we are going to hear them at all. I once received a letter from a friend who had his first college teaching job. He said that things were going along quite well, except for the president, a man noted for his dictatorial tendencies. "He keeps getting himself confused with God," my friend wrote. And this was precisely the problem with both David and Ahab. David wanted a person, Ahab wanted some property. And because they had access to power and were surrounded with loyal subordinates who followed orders without asking questions, it was a simple matter to get what they wanted, even though both the quest for Bathsheba and the quest for the vegetable garden ended up in murder.

In the biblical tradition, as we have seen, the special obligation of the man who exercises power is a concern for the powerless. But power somehow intoxicates, and clouds the sense of right and wrong so that one may justify intrigue, illegal acts, even murder, on the grounds that he is doing it for "*Fuehrer, Volk, und Vaterland,*" or maybe for "national security purposes." When those who wield power in our time tend toward confusing themselves with God, the prophetic word still stands as a reminder that there is a God who watches over the powerless and who calls those who are in positions of power to responsibility, and even to judgment.

This means that religion has something to do with politics, as both David and Ahab discovered. And perhaps the politics of ancient Samaria or Jerusalem are really not so far removed from the politics of Moscow, Paris, or Washington. Do we as a nation know what it is to become arrogant, proud, even ruthless in our exercise of power? Then the prophetic "Have you killed and also taken possession?" is addressed to us. But there is a good deal of power in the church, too. Do we as a People of God know what it is to enjoy marvelous buildings, propose imaginative programs, initiate impressive budgets, and then forget the powerless in our midst? The unemployed worker, the unwed mother, the underprivileged child, the under-educated Indian or Black, the unwanted old man or old woman? The words from that story of Nathan seem to be aimed at us: "The rich man had very many flocks and herds; but the poor man had nothing . . . ." Or when my own career develops, when I move up the ladder, is it possible that I can view the framing of Naboth or hear Nathan's parable and shake my head and point my finger—but never notice how my own pride and arrogance grow in proportion to each new promotion? The words of the prophet remain a Word from God. When you or I as citizens, members of God's family, or individuals have forgotten the powerless, that prophetic word has our name on it: "You are the man!" Or the church, or the nation.

5

Amos and the Affluent Society

On Mississippi River Boulevard in St. Paul, Minnesota, is a beautiful Jewish synagogue named Temple of Aaron. On one of the outside walls, in view of the Mississippi, is a quotation from the prophet Amos: "Let justice well up as waters, and righteousness as a mighty stream." These words in this place capture the essence of the preaching of Amos in an unforgettable manner. The prophetic words continue to call for justice and righteousness to roll through the land, like the waters of the mighty Mississippi! But now let us look at the situation to which these words were first addressed.

AFFLUENCE IN ISRAEL

The first verse of the book of Amos gives us the editor's introduction to the preaching of the prophet:

> The words of Amos, who was among the shepherds of Tekoa, which he saw concerning Israel in the days of Uzziah king of Judah and in the days of Jeroboam the son of Joash, king of Israel, two years before the earthquake. (Amos 1:1)

Before we listen to the words of Amos, the Bible itself insists that we acquaint ourselves with the time when he lived, the days when Uzziah was king of Judah (783–742 B.C.) and Jeroboam king of Israel (786–746 B.C.). If the earthquake mentioned is to be dated around 760 B.C., as seems likely, Amos did his preaching shortly before that date.[1]

These were good years for both Israel and Judah. The international situation was favorable for these small nations on the eastern coast of the Mediterranean. After some warfare in the years just preceding Uzziah and Jeroboam (2 Kings 14:1–22), Israel and Judah were at peace with one another. Egypt was not exercising any influence in the area. Syria had been a nuisance throughout the ninth century, and so when the Assyrian armies crushed Damascus in about 802 B.C., this came as good news to Israel and Judah. Then the years from 783–746 B.C. saw a succession of weak rulers in Assyria, who were not able to maintain any hold on these nations in the the west. Assyrian weakness was matched by strength in both northern and southern kingdoms, with Jeroboam and Uzziah providing able leadership for a period of about forty years. The biblical historian notes that Jeroboam extended the borders of Israel as far north as Solomon had (2 Kings 14:25). Uzziah's accomplishments are described in considerable detail and summarized in the statement that "his fame spread far. . . ." (2 Chron. 26:1–15) Peace had finally come, it seemed, in a manner that had not been experienced since the glorious days of David and Solomon!

This time of peace was matched by prosperity in both kingdoms. Archaeology provides some evidence for this, in the eighth-century buildings with ivory inlays which have been unearthed at Samaria, the capital of the northern kingdom.[2] But the best evidence for the situation in Israel comes from the book of Amos itself. The prophet addresses a situation where business is good and the economy vigorous (8:5). Farmers are raising sheep and cattle (6:4) and planting vineyards (5:11). New homes are being built, lavishly decorated with ivory, with some citizens able to afford separate resi dences for summer and winter (3:15). Inside these beautiful dwellings are those who live in luxury, enjoying their leisure with plenty of food, wine by the bowlful, expensive perfumes, and novel music (6:4–6). Religion is prospering, too. Worshipers flock to the shrines at places like Bethel and Gilgal, busying themselves with the offering of sacrifices and the singing of hymns (4:4 f.; 5:21–23).

These were good times, indeed! Now well into the second hundred years of their national existence, the citizens of Israel were quite satisfied with themselves, their nation, and their God. And they looked forward to an even greater time in the future, when the "Day of the Lord" would come and God would make his chosen people victorious over all their enemies and truly establish them as the first of all the nations on the earth (5:18; cf. 6:1).

But then it happened. One day at the royal chapel in Bethel, the place where the king himself worshiped, a sheepherder and farmer from the Judean town of Tekoa appeared. In the midst of the smell of the sacrifices and the sound of the hymns came the voice of one who spoke in the manner of a messenger from God. He began, "Thus says the Lord . . . "

AMOS THE MAN

Who was this man whose abrasive words interrupted the smooth operation of the sanctuary at Bethel? His name was Amos. The Bible really doesn't tell us much about him. As with all the prophets, it is the message and not the man that is of primary importance. But we do learn, first of all, that he was neither on the clergy roster nor on any kind of payroll of the religious establishment. This is clear from the encounter between Amos and Amaziah, the priest who was in charge of the king's chapel (7:10–17). Amos had been saying some things that made him a prime candidate for investigation by the Committee on Anti-Israelite Activities! The king would die, and the citizens would be taken off into exile, announced this Tekoan sheepherder turned prophet! After getting off a report to the king, Amaziah wheeled on Amos, calling him a "seer" and telling him to peddle his prophecies back home where he came from, "but never again prophesy at Bethel, for it is the king's sanctuary. . . ." (7:13) Amos understood. The priest thought that he was one of that core of professional religionists who hung around the court, one of those "yes-men" who could be counted upon to bless new buildings, pray at banquets, generally endorse national policy and assure the king that God was on his side. These court "prophets" had been on hand at least since the time of Ahab in the ninth century (1 Kings 22:5 f., 10–12). Groups of them could be called the "sons of the prophets." (Cf. 2 Kings 2:5, 15.) Amos immediately disassociated himself from any such "professionals." "I am no prophet, nor one of the sons of the prophets," he said (7:14, R.S.V. margin).

Amos identified himself as a layman, a sheepherder, and one who cared for sycamore trees (7:14). In our day, we would call him a farmer or better yet, a rancher. His hometown was Tekoa (1:1), a village some ten miles south of Jerusalem. Tekoa is also mentioned as the home of a certain "wise woman" who once told a parable to King David, much in the manner of Nathan's parable (2 Sam. 14:1–20). It is therefore possible that this town was a center for the kind of wisdom teaching which we find in the book of Proverbs. In any case, the love which Amos has for typical "wisdom" devices such as numerical sayings (chapters 1 and 2; cf. Prov. 30:15–31), comparisons (2:9; 5:19, 24; 9:9, etc.) and didactic questions (3:3–6) leads us to believe that he was well acquainted with the kind of wisdom instruction which Proverbs exemplifies. And we recall from our discussion in Chapter 3 above that an important theme in this material was a concern for the powerless.

As we listen to his preaching, we discover more about Amos. He was informed about the events of international politics and commented upon these events in the lengthy speech which we find in the first two chapters of the book. Perhaps his work took him to these countries, or he simply may have been an observer of the current political scene. He also knew something about the historical origins of other nations (9:7). Amos viewed the world around him with the eye of the poet, and brought that world into his preaching. He knew the life of the farmer, threshing with modern iron equipment (1:3), harvesting (2:13), despairing over lack of rainfall (4:7 f.) or suffering terrible crop loss (7:1 f.). The hunter catching a bird (3:5), the shepherd grieving over a dead lamb (3:12) or fearful at the roar of a lion (3:8), the carpenter building a wall (7:7), the sound of the trumpet signaling an alarm (3:6), and the sight of sleek cattle grazing in the fields of Bashan (4:1) all furnished the illustrative material for the sermons of Amos.

But what made him a prophet? Certainly not the education which he received in Tekoa, or his keen perceptions about international affairs, or his knack for poetic expression, though all of these were taken up into the service of prophecy. He himself tells us: " . . . the LORD took me from following the flock, and the LORD said to me, 'Go, prophesy to my people Israel.' " (7:15) He was a prophet because God called him to this task. We can gain an insight into the nature of that call as we look at the series of visions which are reported in chapters 7—9. First, Amos sees a pair of frightening events. Locusts devour the crops, and the fires of invading armies consume the land. Amos gets the message: the people of Israel (here called Jacob) are going to be destroyed! In each case he pleads with God, asking him not to let it happen, and the Lord says "It shall not be." (7:1–6) But there is something different about the third vision. Amos sees the Lord standing beside a wall, holding a plumb line. The wall is crooked, and obviously must be torn down. This time Amos is silent. He understands that there is a reason for the coming doom. Like a wall which is out of plumb, Israel does not measure up to her Maker's expectations! (7:7–9) In a fourth vision he sees a basket of summer fruit, in Hebrew a "*qayits.*" In a grim play on words, he hears the Lord say that the end (Hebrew "*qets*") has come upon this people! (8:1–3) Finally, Amos sees the temple itself destroyed. Those people who manage to escape the disaster will find no place to hide from the wrath which is to come (9:1–4). After experiencing this series of frightening visions, Amos knew what was about to happen to the people to the north. Doom and destruction! But what was he to do?

God had shown him what was wrong with this people and what was in store for them. God had spoken to him. And now he felt compelled to speak to the people, as a messenger from the Lord. Jeremiah would one day call this compulsion " 'a burning fire shut up in my bones.' " (Jer. 20:9) Amos described it in terms drawn from his life as a shepherd. On an occasion where someone seems to have challenged his right to speak, he gave to his audience a series of cause and effect relationships (3:3–8). People meet, he said, because they have an appointment; lions roar because they have captured their prey; birds fall to the ground because they have been trapped; citizens are afraid because the alarm trumpet has sounded; evil comes upon a city because the Lord does it. His hearers would agree with all that! The effect always follows the cause. Then Amos climaxes the series with two final cause/effect relationships. A lion roars, and a man can't help but fear! The Lord speaks, and one can't help but prophesy!

And so God called this layman, this rancher from Tekoa, to go and preach. He was to deliver a message to that confident and affluent society to the north. Amos knew he had to say something. Now let us listen to what he had to say.

REMINDER OF WHAT GOD HAS DONE

I recall being asked to review a new Sunday School book which was designed to introduce the Old Testament to sixth

graders. One of the early lessons was making the point that
there are various types of literature in the Old Testament, and
there was a short quiz with it. Various literary materials were
pictured, and the student was supposed to associate each with
a part of the Bible. I mentally filled in the blanks: a hymn
book, Psalms; a page of wise sayings from an almanac, Proverbs; a book of laws, Leviticus and others. But there was one I
could not figure out. It was the weather forecast section from
a newspaper. What did that have to do with the Bible? Finally
I looked up the answer and discovered that the weather
predictions were supposed to remind the reader of the
prophets! Now the prophets were of course concerned with
the future. But not exclusively, or even mainly. They were
also concerned with the past, and most of all with the present.

When Amos speaks to his audiences about the past, he
reminds them of what God has done for them. Listen to the
short oracle in Amos 3:1–2:

> Hear this word that the LORD has spoken against you,
> O people of Israel, against the whole family which
> I brought up out of the land of Egypt:
> "You only have I known of all the families of the earth;
>   therefore I will punish you for all your iniquities."

Remember, says the prophet, that God delivered you from
Egypt and made your life as a nation possible! And then he
talks about the special relationship that God has with this
people. The language, "You only have I known," is familiar
from the language of treaties in the ancient world and has the
sense of entering into a special covenant relationship with
someone. But then comes the shocking note. Along with the
special privilege of being a People of God went special responsibilities. And since the people have not responded as
they ought, they can expect punishment!

Listen to another reminder of what God has done for his
people; the prophet is speaking as God's messenger:

"Also I brought you up out of the land of Egypt,
and led you forty years in the wilderness,
to possess the land of the Amorite." (2:10)

Remember what God has done for you! The Exodus, the guidance in the wilderness, and the conquest of the land of Palestine. The words of the prophet in the verse just preceding expand upon the conquest theme:

"Yet I destroyed the Amorite before them,
whose height was like the height of the cedars,
and who was as strong as the oaks;
I destroyed his fruit above, and his roots beneath." (2:9)

Finally, there is another context in which the prophet reminds his hearers of what God has done for them. This text gives us a hint of the majesty and power of the God of Amos. He has not only acted in the history of Israel, but he has acted in the history of other nations as well! Speaking again as the Lord's messenger the prophet says,

"Did I not bring up Israel from the land of Egypt,
and the Philistines from Caphtor
and the Syrians from Kir?" (9:7)

When we hear the prophet reminding his audience of their special relationship to God, and reminding them what their God has done for them in the Exodus and other events, we realize that this way of talking about God and people is nothing new. The prophet is standing squarely in the tradition of Moses, with the Sinai covenant sealing the *relationship* between God and people, the preface to the commandments sounding the *reminder* of what God has done, and the Ten Commandments themselves spelling out the expected *response* of the people, toward God and toward one another. But what of that response in the Israel that Amos saw? There was the real target of the prophet's preaching.

RESPONSE TOWARD GOD

Amos had something to say about the people's relationship to God. We remember that the Ten Commandments began by indicating how the covenant people were expected to respond toward God, which we might call the vertical dimension of their response. They were to have no other gods, make no images of God, not take his name in vain, and remember the sabbath day (Exod. 20:3–11). And Israel had not forgotten about God. On the contrary, the businessmen closed their shops on the sabbath (8:5) and the shrines were busy places (4:4 f.; 5:21–23). A pollster would have found a high degree of religious activity in the Israel of those days! But underneath it all, something was wrong.

If you travel about Israel today and are interested in looking for ancient biblical sites, you will often discover a sign which says, *Maqom Qadosh*, that is, "Holy Place." And if there ever was a holy place in the Israel of the time of Amos, it was at Bethel. There Jacob had dreamed his dream about a ladder reaching to heaven. When he awoke he said, "This is none other than the house of God," and gave the place its name; in Hebrew "Beth" is house, and "El" is God (Gen. 28:10—22). The first of the kings in the north made Bethel one of the two centers for worship (1 Kings 12:26—33), and we have seen that in the days of Amos it was a royal sanctuary (Amos 7:13). Amos visited Bethel and had some things to say about the worship that was going on there.

An analogy from our own manner of worship might help us to understand his words. At the beginning of the Sunday morning service in churches which follow a liturgical tradition is a part called the "Introit." The word means entry, and it originally referred to the priest entering the altar area as the service began. Nowadays it functions as a call to worship. As an example, the Introit for the twenty-fifth Sunday after Pentecost begins, "O come, let us worship and bow down, let us kneel before the LORD, our Maker!"[3] The reader will recognize that these words are taken from Psalm 95, where they functioned in exactly the same way, to call the people of ancient Israel to worship. If we are to catch the impact of the words of Amos at Bethel, we ought to imagine him delivering them at a point where one would expect an "introit" or call to worship. He began, "Come to Bethel . . . " One would expect, "and worship the Lord," or something similar to follow. But listen:

> "Come to Bethel, and transgress;
>> to Gilgal, and multiply transgression;
> bring your sacrifices every morning,
>> your tithes every three days;
> offer a sacrifice of thanksgiving of that which is leavened,
>> and proclaim freewill offerings, publish them;
> for so you love to do, O people of Israel!"says the Lord God.

(Amos 4:4–5)

Amos was mocking the call of the priests. "Come to church . . . and sin!" he said. A call to worship might continue by giving a reason for worship; in the Introit we have examined, from Psalm 95, the reason is, "For he is our God, and we are the people of his pasture, and the sheep of his hand." But note the reason in the "call to worship" which Amos delivers! "For so you love to do. . . " With biting sarcasm, the prophet says that what is going on at Bethel is not worship of God, but worship of self, motivated by a love for ceremony, and the publicity resulting from contributions made to the religious establishment! And the final, "says the Lord God" identifies the word as a word from God, spoken by his messenger.

But why should the worship that these people carried on be so unacceptable to God? That question is answered as we listen to another word from Amos, delivered in the first-person style of the messenger from God. We should imagine the prophet speaking at another gathering of the people for worship, perhaps again at Bethel:

"I hate, I despise your feasts,
   and I take no delight in your solemn assemblies.
Even though you offer me your burnt offerings and cereal offerings,
   I will not accept them,
and the peace offerings of your fatted beasts
   I will not look upon.
Take away from me the noise of your songs;
   to the melody of your harps I will not listen.
But let justice roll down like waters,
   and righteousness like an ever-flowing stream."
                          (5:21–24)

The Hebrew of verse 21 reads literally, "I don't like the smell of your solemn assemblies." Thus the prophet speaking in God's name says, "I don't like the smell (21), the sight (22), or the sound (23) of all these goings-on at the sanctuary!" The worship of this people is totally rejected! And why? Not because feast days are not properly observed, sacrifices are not rightly offered, or because the Bethel choirs are out of tune. Not at all. The problem was not with what happened in the sanctuary on the sabbath, but with what happened, or failed to happen, outside the sanctuary, on the other days of the week. Perhaps Amos was thinking of a bit of wisdom instruction he had picked up, "To do righteousness and justice is more acceptable to the LORD than sacrifice." (Prov. 21:3) At any rate, he made it clear that a religion which never gets out of "holy places" is a religion wholly unacceptable to God! The Lord, said Amos, wants a religion that results in justice and righteousness! But now let us see just what the prophet meant by this.

RESPONSE TOWARD THE POWERLESS

If the prophet had things to say about the people's relationship to God, he had more to say about their relationships with one another. The Ten Commandments had indicated that there was a horizontal dimension to the response expected from the covenant people, too. They were to respond to what God had done for them by living out their social relationships in a certain way (Exod. 20:12–17), and Amos had much to say about these relationships in Israel.

Few prophetic sermons have the power of the long one recorded in Amos 1:3—2:16. In order to get the full impact of it, I suggest that you, the reader, take a pencil and circle the names of the eight nations mentioned in the sermon and then locate each of them on a map, such as is found in the back of most Bibles. I suggest that you also identify each of the following elements in the first seven parts (1:3—2:5) of the prophet's sermon;

1. Messenger formula: (Thus says the LORD)
2. Accusation
   a. General: For three transgressions of _____and for four, I will not revoke the punishment . . .
   b. Specific: because they _____
3. Announcement of Punishment: So I will send/kindle a fire . . .
4. Concluding messenger formula: says the LORD GOD (missing in Tyre, Edom, and Judah oracles)

The text does not indicate where this long sermon was delivered, though Bethel seems a likely place. We do know that it was preached to people of Israel; notice the switch to the second-person "you" form of address starting with Amos 2:10. And now try to put yourself in the position of an Israelite hearing this sermon. It would be best if you would read it aloud because like all sermons, it was designed to be heard, not read. The sound of sacrifices and songs is interrupted by the announcement, "Thus says the Lord." Who is that man? You don't recognize him. But he begins by announcing the Lord's punishment upon Damascus. You listen with interest and even nod in agreement, because the Syrians have long been enemies of your country! He continues by announcing

punishment upon Gaza and Tyre. Again you agree, and
perhaps even applaud, approving of this theology which sees
the Lord as God of all the nations, not just Israel! Then he has
oracles to deliver against the nations of Edom, Ammon (the
name survives in the modern Amman, capital of Jordan), and
Moab. By this time you join the crowd in cheering the prophet
after each new denunciation of these foreigners! The prophet
has his audience with him, hanging on each word! Who will be
next? But listen. The next announcement of doom is for
Judah, just to the south! With this, you become a bit uneasy,
and an unnatural silence falls upon the crowd. Finally the
prophet inserts your own nation, Israel, into the formula, and
the simple format is sprung. You hear the messenger formula
and general accusation, but then the specific accusations are
much expanded (2:6b–12) as is the announcement of punishment (2:13–16). Then the sermon ends with the short concluding "says the LORD."

But what were the accusations against the people of
Israel? In contrast to those against the other nations (except
for Judah) which had to do with war crimes, these accusations
have to do with social ills within Israel herself. Amos names
five instances of oppression of the powerless: 1. The righteous
but needy person is sold as a slave, because he owes some
silver or even such a little thing as a pair of sandals (this seems
to be the sense of 2:6b). Compare the story of the poor widow
who has to sell her two sons because she cannot pay her debts
(2 Kings 4:1–7)! 2. The poor and afflicted man is not given a
fair shake in the courts (this is the sense of "turn aside the way
of . . . " in 2:7a). 3. The person of the young woman is not
respected, when both a son and his father have sexual relationships with her (2:7b; cf. Lev. 18:15). 4. The clothing which
a poor man gave as security for a debt has not been returned,
contrary to ancient Israelite law (Exod. 22:26 f.). 5. Money
paid in fines (Exod. 21:22; Deut. 22:19) is being used for
partying (2:8b). In sum, the powerless are being trampled into

the dust of the earth, contrary to everything expected of the People of God as expressed in legal, wisdom and psalm traditions! And now, says Amos, those who have so oppressed will themselves be pressed—pressed down, like the ground over which a heavily loaded wagon rolls! (2:13)

Amos had more to say about the administration of justice in Israel's courts, in several short oracles which we find in chapter five. To understand them, we should have something of an idea of how courts in ancient Israel functioned. The homes and shops comprised the town or city, and were surrounded by a wall which provided security. The center of activity would be the city gate (or gates) through which the farmers passed as they went to work in the fields in the morning, and as they returned in the evenings. When someone had a complaint to make, perhaps concerning a theft, rights to a well, or a boundary dispute, or when he had a matter which had to be settled by proper legal means, he went to the gate and called together ten men to make up a court, which would then make the legal decision. (The interested reader can find an example of this procedure in the fourth chapter of Ruth.) Thus when passages like Proverbs 22:22, or Amos 5:10, 12, or 15 talk about "the gate" or "justice in the gate," they are talking about the gate as the place where the court assembled and justice was administered.

In one short saying from Amos, the prophet simply calls for his hearers to "establish justice in the gate," that is, to make the right decisions in the courts (5:15, as part of 5:14 f.). But in two oracles, the prophet accuses the people of corruption in their courts, and announces to them that they shall be punished for this corruption. The first is found in 5:7, together with verses 10 and 11. We skip around verses 8 and 9 because they are verses from a hymn (note also 4:13 and 9:5 f.) and should be considered separately.[4] The piece then reads,

> Woe to those who turn justice to wormwood,[5]
> and cast down righteousness to the earth!

> They hate him who reproves in the gate,
>> and they abhor him who speaks the truth.
> Therefore because you trample upon the poor
>> and take from him exactions of wheat,
> you have built houses of hewn stone,
>> but you shall not dwell in them;
> you have planted pleasant vineyards,
>> but you shall not drink their wine.

The prophet accuses the citizenry of turning justice to poison, hating the man who speaks the truth in court, and charging exorbitant rent of the poor farmer. Then he announces that because of this oppression of the powerless, the plans of the wealthy will be frustrated. They will never live in those lavish homes, nor will they drink the wine of those luxuriant vineyards!

Another prophetic word about the court system is found in 5:12. After a general accusation, Amos lists three complaints about the courts:

> For I know how many are your transgressions,
>> and how great are your sins—
> you who afflict the righteous,
>> who take a bribe,
> and turn aside the needy in the gate.

We have seen that in Amos an accusation is ordinarily coupled with an announcement of future punishment (chapters 1 and 2; 5:7, 10 f.). After the accusation in verse 12 is a short observation which sounds like it is from the hand of one assembling the Amos oracles (5:13) and then a piece complete in itself (5:14 f.). Verses 16 and 17 furnish the announcement of punishment and should be linked with verse 12. After the messenger formula, the prophet announces that the day is coming when weeping, wailing, and the sounds of funerals will fill the land (5:16 f.).

The courts discriminated against the powerless. But what about the situation downtown? In a word delivered to the businessmen, Amos accused them of just the same kind of oppression:

> Hear this, you who trample upon the needy,
>   and bring the poor of the land to an end. (8:4)

He continued by quoting what he knew was in their hearts, if not on their lips:

> saying, "When will the new moon be over,
>   that we may sell grain?
> And the sabbath,
>   that we may offer wheat for sale,
> that we may make the ephah small and the shekel great,
>   and deal deceitfully with false balances,
> that we may buy the poor for silver
>   and the needy for a pair of sandals,
> and sell the refuse of the wheat?" (8:5 f.)

Outwardly, these merchants seemed quite religious indeed, closing their shops on sabbaths and religious holidays. But watch out for them when they open up again! Buy a bushel of wheat, (the ephah was a measure roughly equal to our bushel), and you'll discover the merchant's bushel basket was undersize! Sell him some grain, and he'll cheat you with crooked scales! (Note Deut. 25:13–16; Lev. 19:35 f.; and Prov. 20:10.) And the poor are bought and sold as slaves, treated like property, not as persons. Because of such corruption in the marketplace, the prophet as God's messenger again announces that doomsday is coming! (8:7 f.)

This shepherd from Tekoa had delivered some harsh words to the men who served in the courts and who bought and sold in their shops. But he had something to say to the women of Israel, too! They are also considered as persons responsible for what has happened to the powerless in Israel. The prophet must have been observing them as they moved about the marketplaces of Samaria, shopping and stopping on occasion to sip a bit of wine. A comparison came to his cattleman's mind: the cows grazing in the sunny pasturelands of Bashan, an area famous for its sleek, well-fed cattle (Ezek. 39:18; Deut. 32:14). Then he delivered a word from God which showed that he considered these women of the capital city to be responsible persons; in fact as persons who with their husbands were responsible for what was happening to the poor in their society:

"Hear this word, you cows of Bashan,
      who are in the mountain of Samaria,
who oppress the poor, who crush the needy,
      who say to their husbands, 'Bring, that we may drink!' "
                                                              (4:1)

The oracle continues in the fashion we have noted elsewhere, with an announcement of future punishment following upon this accusation. These creatures will soon leave the security of Samaritan society, strung out single file and being led through the holes which will be knocked in the city's walls! (4:2 f.)

Finally, we shall listen to a word from Amos which well summarizes what the prophet had to say. Chapter 6:1–7 records a prophetic "woe saying," which means that the prophet is speaking in a manner which imitates the cry of the mourner at a funeral, thus announcing doom and death. It also falls into the pattern that we have noted in each of the other oracles we have examined, with an accusation (1–6) providing the grounds for an announcement of future punishment (7). Amos pronounces a woe upon the leadership in the capital cities of both Jerusalem (located on Mt. Zion) and Samaria, a leadership which is at ease and arrogant, confident that theirs is the first of the nations of the world:

"Woe to those who are at ease in Zion,
      and to those who feel secure on the mountain of Samaria,
the notable men of the first of the nations,
      to whom the house of Israel come!" (6:1)

He continues with words which continue to express this arrogance, and which should be understood as a quotation from those leaders.[6] They say, "Look at the nations around us. Certainly we are better than they, and we have more territory!" (6:2)

Then the prophet pronounces a woe upon the upper class which has developed in Israel during the nearly two hundred years of its national life. Listen to the way in which the prophet describes the luxury which the leadership enjoys, and then climaxes that description with a jarring statement about the nation Israel, here named "Joseph":

"Woe to those who lie upon beds of ivory,
    and stretch themselves upon their couches,
and eat lambs from the flock,
    and calves from the midst of the stall;
who sing idle songs to the sound of the harp,
    and like David invent for themselves instruments of music;
who drink wine in bowls,
    and anoint themselves with the finest oils,
but are not grieved over the ruin of Joseph!"

(6:4–6; emphasis added)

The oracle ends with an announcement of future doom which picks up the themes of both the arrogance and affluence of the prophet's hearers:

"Therefore they shall now be the first of those
    to go into exile,
and the revelry of those who stretch themselves shall pass away."

(6:7)

Those who say they are the first will be the first—the first to go into exile! And the affluence will be no more. At ease, arrogant, affluent—and unconcerned about their nation! So the prophet described those in positions of wealth and power, in this nation which had forgotten its powerless.

AMOS, AFFLUENCE, AND BICENTENNIALS

We have heard the prophet remind Israel of what God had done for them in their past, and accuse them of failure to respond as they ought to have in the present. But what of this people's future? Amos had seen it in his vision, "The end has come upon my people Israel." (8:2) And though he did exhort his hearers to live as worthy People of God (5:14 f.), the central message of his preaching was accusation coupled with an announcement of future doom, in the manner of the oracles we have heard in the preceding section. The end did come. In 922 B.C. Israel, the northern kingdom, had its beginning as an independent nation. And in 722 B.C., just a bicentennial later, the proud city of Samaria fell to the armies of Assyria (2 Kings 17) and the northern kingdom was no more.

But if we call ourselves a People of God, still living under the authority of the prophetic word, we need to hear the preaching of Amos, too. What of the reminder of what God has done? We no longer celebrate the Exodus from Egypt, though our Jewish neighbor still does. But we are reminded week by week of another deliverance, a "New Exodus," from the bondage of sin, death, and the power of the devil. This is the Good News of what God has done through our Lord and Savior, Jesus Christ. And the God who has delivered us continues to "bless us on our way, with countless gifts of love" as we sing in our hymns and he gives us such daily bread as "food and clothing, home and property, work and income, a devoted family, an orderly community, good government, favorable weather, peace and health, a good name, and true friends and neighbors," as we learn in our catechism. God has given us much!

And what of our response toward God? We can point to churches no less magnificent than that royal chapel at Bethel, churches filled with the music of Bach or Gabrieli and the art of Michelangelo. Statistics and the new spirit among the young would tend to show that we are quite a religious nation, indeed. We preface even our movies with advertisements to attend "the church of your choice." But is it possible that all of this religious activity can turn out to be nothing more than the "noise of solemn assemblies"? Is it possible that God himself might reject the sight and the sound of our weekly worship? According to Amos it is possible, though such a thought makes us very uncomfortable indeed. But when is religion not acceptable to God? We might express the message of Amos this way: *There can be no dichotomy between religion and life.* The people of Israel had divided their lives into two compartments. One was labeled "religion" and meant attending services, singing hymns, tithing, and closing their shops on the sabbath. The other was marked "life," and as we have seen, this included oppression of the powerless in the courts and marketplace, and an attitude of complacent unconcern. A convenient dichotomy indeed! Religion in one compartment, the rest of life in another, and the two are kept quite separate! I recall a banner at a college which announced a week as "Religion and Life Week." But then someone changed it, striking out the "and" so that it read "Religion *in* Life Week." Completely in the spirit of Amos! Perhaps a personal recollection will make the point clear. I remember as a boy of maybe twelve years going pheasant hunting, along with my father and a group of farmers. The smell of the crisp fall day, the sound of shotguns in distant cornfields, all remain vivid memories. After an afternoon of hiking through the fields there was that good feeling of sitting around with the men and listening to their conversation. One of the farmers said that he needed to buy a new tractor. "Where should I buy it?" he wondered. "Why not buy it from Pete?" said someone, "after all he belongs to our church." Then another old fellow took the stub of a cigar out of his mouth and picked up the conversation. "Ya, he belongs to your church all right. In fact he goes to church twice each Sunday. But you'd better watch out for him in his implement shop on Monday morning! He'll take you for everything you've got!" This implement dealer had made a dichotomy between his religion and his life, keeping the two quite separate. And that farmer with the cigar knew that there was something wrong with a religion which didn't get out of the sanctuary and into the shops and onto the streets.

The major concern of Amos was with the response of the people of Israel toward the powerless in their midst. We have seen that he was saying nothing new, but simply reminding his hearers that *the People of God are expected to show a concern for the powerless.* And now the words of the prophet begin to speak to us as a People of God, but also as a people who live as citizens of a political nation that we love dearly. Amos spoke of discrimination against the needy in the courts. Will the young Indian, Black or poor man get the same kind of justice as the wealthy rancher or businessman in our own courts? Amos spoke of dishonesty downtown; do we not know what it is to say "but business is business!" We are concerned about the liberation of women in our society; Amos reminds us of the social responsibility which women share. And then there are the words addressed to those who are "at ease" and "secure," confident that theirs is "the first of the nations." (6:1–7) They enjoy elegant furnishings, appreciate fine music, and know how to select the right wines. They wouldn't think of oppressing a poor man or cheating a widow. But they aren't really concerned about them, either. They don't care about what is happening to their country, and don't want to get mixed up in politics. And in a few years after Amos spoke to them, just two hundred years after their nation began, it was all over for Israel.

Amos announced Israel's bicentennial. But for them, it was a day of gloom, with no brightness in it. Though we don't want his words any more than those citizens of Samaria did, perhaps he has something to say to us, at this time just past our own nation's bicentennial. He warns us that a nation which lives in quadraphonic affluence coupled with indifference toward the powerless is a nation which has no future. He asks us as a People of God to grieve over the "ruin of Joseph," over the injustice in our own nation. He calls us out of indifference to concern; out of arrogance to repentance. Then by the grace of the God in whom our fathers trusted, and in whom we trust, justice may begin to roll down like waters, and righteousness like an everflowing stream.

6

Advocates for the Powerless

Isaiah is probably the best known of all the biblical prophets. From the simplest program in a country parish to the most sophisticated production in a metropolitan music hall, his words are heard each Christmas time: "For to us a Child is born . . . ." (9:6) And this prophet from Judah belongs to all the nations of the world. Words from Isaiah are inscribed on the United Nations building in New York City, expressing mankind's universal hope for peace:

And they shall beat their swords into plowshares,
    and their spears into pruning hooks;
nation shall not lift up sword against nation,
    neither shall they learn war any more. (2:4b)

Isaiah had much to say about the Messiah and the Messianic Age. But he also called for justice to be established in the land, with all the passion of an Amos. We shall begin by listening to his Song of the Vineyard, to be found in Isaiah 5:1–7.

THE CALM BEFORE THE STORM

Once again, the compiler of this prophetic book insists that we hear the prophet in his own historical setting:

The vision of Isaiah the son of Amoz, which he saw concerning Judah and Jerusalem in the days of Uzziah, Jotham, Ahaz, and Hezekiah, kings of Judah. (Isa. 1:1)

Isaiah had an unusually long career as a prophet in the southern kingdom. If his call came in the year that Uzziah died (742 B.C.; 6:1) and if he worked during the reign of Hezekiah (715–687 B.C.), this means that he played an active part in the life of his nation for some fifty years. The Song of the Vineyard and most of the prophetic sermons to which we shall listen in this chapter fit best into the first period of Isaiah's ministry, soon after his call in 742 B.C. and before the struggles with Syria and Israel began in 735 B.C. Jotham was king in Judah during these years (2 Kings 15:32–38).

The international situation during these earliest years of Isaiah's activity allowed Judah a few more years of independence. Egypt was not exercising any influence in the area. Israel and Syria had not yet invaded Judah in their attempt to force Judah into an anti-Assyrian coalition (2 Kings 16:5 ff; Isa. 7:1 ff.). And though Assyria was beginning her revival under the powerful Tiglath-pileser III (745–727 B.C.), Judah would not come under her control until Ahaz sold out his nation's freedom in 735 B.C. For Judah it was a time of calm before the storm.

Internally, the nation continued to enjoy the prosperity brought about by Uzziah. Something of the spirit of the times is reflected in sayings of Isaiah which seem to come from this period. The wealthy are buying up small farms and consolidating them into big ones, as they join house to house, and add field to field (5:8). There are those in this society, too, who revel in luxury, with live music and wine accompanying their all-night parties (5:11 f.). We even catch a glimpse of the ladies of Jerusalem. The prophet has seen them, as they

> . . . walk with outstretched necks, glancing wantonly with their eyes, mincing along as they go, tinkling with their feet. . . . (3:16)

He catalogs their clothing with a description that would make the most sophisticated twentieth-century socialite envious:

> . . . the finery of the anklets, the headbands, and the crescents; the pendants, the bracelets, and the scarfs; the headdresses, the armlets, the sashes, the perfume boxes, and the amulets; the signet rings and nose rings; the festal robes, the mantles, the cloaks, and the handbags; the garments of gauze, the linen garments, the turbans, and the veils. (3:18–23)

If dress is an indicator of affluence, these were good times indeed!

What about religion during these days? One thing is certain. The sanctuaries were busy places. Attendance at worship services was at a high point! The prophet hints at the multitude of sacrifices, the burnt offerings of rams, the fat of fed beasts, the blood of bulls, lambs, he-goats, all part of Judah's sacrificial system (1:11). And the holy days were being observed with the proper ceremonies and celebrations (1:13 f.).

Jerusalem, just past mid-eighth century B.C. The economy booming, the elite basking in the prosperity of the Uzziah years, and the ecclesiastical institutions buzzing with sacrifices and songs. But beneath it all, something was wrong. There was a sickness eating away at the heart of the nation. Amos had seen it in Israel; Isaiah diagnosed it in Judah. But how to get his people to realize it, before it was too late?

THE SONG OF THE VINEYARD

We might imagine a festival celebrating the harvesting of the vineyards during these good years, somewhere in the neighborhood of Jerusalem. There would be singing, dancing, and wine for all (cf. Judg. 9:27). In the midst of the festivities the young man Isaiah stepped forward. "Let me sing a song," he said, "a song about my friend and his vineyard." And so he began, perhaps to the accompaniment of the eighth-century equivalent of a folk singer's guitar:

> Let me sing about my friend,
> > a song about my friend and his vineyard:
>
> My friend had a vineyard on a very fertile hill.[1]
> He digged it and cleared it of stones,
> > and planted it with choice vines;
>
> he built a watchtower in the midst of it,
> > and hewed out a wine vat in it;
>
> and he looked for it to yield grapes,
> > but it yielded wild grapes. (5:1–2)

The crowd began to quiet down and the prophet had his audience. An interesting folk ballad, about a farmer who did everything he could for a vineyard. After his work of digging, clearing stones, and building a tower so that the vineyard could be guarded during harvest time, he expected some fine fruits. But his expectations were disappointed. The yield was nothing but worthless, wild grapes! One might expect such from the field of a lazy man (cf. Prov. 24:30–34), but not from a vineyard which had enjoyed such care! But listen! The prophet is still singing, now asking for some audience participation. He takes the role of the "friend," and asks his listeners to play the role of a jury, judging a legal case:

> And now, O inhabitants of Jerusalem and men of Judah,
> > judge, I pray you, between me and my vineyard.
>
> What more was there to do for my vineyard,
> > that I have not done in it?
>
> When I looked for it to yield grapes,
> > why did it yield wild grapes? (5:3–4)

Clearly, the "jury" would decide that the "friend" was entirely without fault. There was nothing more he could have done for that vineyard! Then, like a refrain, the prophet repeats the statement of disappointed expectations, this time in the first-person "I" form (5:4b). But the song continues, with a shift into the future tense:

> And now I will tell you what I will do to my vineyard.
> I will remove its hedge, and it shall be devoured;
> I will break down its wall,
>   and it shall be trampled down.
> I will make it a waste;
>   it shall not be pruned or hoed,
>   and briers and thorns shall grow up;
> I will also command the clouds
>   that they rain no rain upon it. (5:5–6)

Again like one pronouncing a sentence in a law court, the "friend" announces what he will do to this unproductive vineyard. Its special protection will be removed, and he will simply stop caring for it. A just sentence, the audience no doubt agrees! But wait. There is more to this song about a vineyard:

> For the vineyard of the Lord of hosts
>   is the house of Israel,
> and the men of Judah
>   are his pleasant planting; (5:7a)

The prophet has tricked his audience into condemning themselves, when they condemned the vineyard! The song concludes as the statement of disappointed expectations is picked up a third time, and the ending is given a special punch with a pair of puns:

> and he looked for justice [mišpāṭ in Hebrew],
>   but behold, bloodshed [miśpāḥ];
> for righteousness [ṣᵉʿāqāh],
>   but behold, a cry! [ṣᵉʿāqāh] (5:7b)

The puns give the song an added dramatic force. We might reproduce them in English with "justice—just vice" and "righteousness—rottenness," or something similar. Anyway, the message of the song was clear! This was no mere ballad, but a prophetic parable designed to trick the hearer into pronouncing judgment on himself, in the manner of Nathan (2 Sam. 12), the wise woman of Tekoa (2 Sam. 14) or the prophet who encountered Ahab (1 Kings 20:35–43). God, like the vineyard keeper, had done much for his people. He had led them out of slavery in Egypt, made covenant with them at Sinai, guided them through the wilderness, and placed them in a good land. Like the vineyard on the fertile hill, they enjoyed his day-by-day blessings in nature as well. But God had expected some response, some fruits of justice and righteousness. What had happened? Only injustice and oppression, like a crop of worthless fruit. And so, said the prophet, God will simply stop caring for this people, and let them be trampled down, worthless and unproductive in justice and righteousness as they are.

DOING JUSTICE, PROPHETIC STYLE

Isaiah's song that day came to a climax when his audience heard him say that God looked for justice and righteousness, but he found only the opposite. These two Hebrew words, mišpāṭ and ṣᵉdāqāh are clearly central to the Song. They indicate what God expects of his people.

But what, precisely, did the prophet mean by mišpāṭ and ṣᵉʿāqāh? Since these two words are right at the heart of our interest in what the prophets have to say about the powerless, we must investigate them rather carefully. Our method will be a simple one. We shall simply listen to each sermon (or summarized sermon) coming from Isaiah where he uses these words, or a word built from the same Hebrew root (a "cognate"; the noun mišpāṭ for example, is derived from the Hebrew verb form šāpaṭ). Then we will put together a picture of what the prophet meant when he used these terms.

The sermons from the prophet Isaiah where these words occur are the following. It would be helpful if you had your Bible at hand and bracketed each of them:

Unit	mišpāṭ *or Cognate*	ṣeʿāqāh *or Cognate*
1:10–17	1:17, 17 (noun and verb)	
1:21–26	1:21, 23	1:21, 26
3:13–15	3:14	
5:1–7	5:7	5:7
5:18–23		5:23, 23, 23 (two nouns, one verb)
9:2–7(Hebrew, 1–6)	9:7 (Hebrew, 6)	9:7 (Hebrew, 6)
10:1–4	10:2	
11:1–9	11:3,4	11:4,5
28:14–22	28:17	28:17

As we listen to these examples of prophetic preaching we discover first of all, that there is a *dynamic* character to the prophetic notion of justice. In the prophetic way of speaking, justice is something one "does."

The sermon recorded in 1:10–17 sounds very much like the preaching of Amos. Speaking as God's messenger, the prophet tells his audience that God rejects their worship because their religion doesn't get out of the sanctuary and into day-by-day living. These pious services are coupled with iniquity (13b) and the very hands that are spread forth in prayer are hands covered with innocent blood (15b). At the conclusion, the prophet addresses some imperatives to his hearers:

> Cease to do evil, learn to do good;
> seek justice [mišpāṭ], correct oppression;
> do justice [the verb, šāpaṭ] for the orphan,
>   take up the cause of the widow.
>   (16b–17, my translation)

One "does justice" when he acts on behalf of the orphan and takes up the cause of the widow.

Isaiah 1:21–26 exhibits a structure that we have encountered in the preaching of Amos, with an accusation (21–23) joined to an announcement of punishment (24b–26) by a messenger formula (24a). The prophet uses an analogy from marriage, comparing once faithful Jerusalem to a wife who has become a faithless whore:

> How the faithful city has become a harlot,
>   she that was full of justice [mišpāṭ]!
> Righteousness [ṣedeq] lodged in her,
>   but now murderers. (1:21)

Jerusalem's political leaders associate with underworld characters, accept bribes, and have forgotten about the powerless:

> Your princes are rebels and companions of thieves.
> Every one loves a bribe and runs after gifts.
> They do not do justice [verb, šāpaṭ] for the orphan,
>   and the widow's cause does not come before them.
>   (1:23, my translation)

Again, justice is something one "does," and here also doing justice involves the orphan and the widow.

A final example from the prophet Micah, a contemporary of Isaiah who also preached in Judah, will provide another example of the dynamic nature of the prophetic notion of justice. The section in Micah 6:6–8 is a short liturgy used as the worshiper entered the temple area, or it could be the prophet imitating such a liturgy. It begins with the worshiper asking a series of questions of the priest:

> "With what shall I come before the LORD,
>   and bow myself before God on high?
> Shall I come before him with burnt offerings,
>   with calves a year old?
> Will the LORD be pleased with thousands of rams,
>   with ten thousands of rivers of oil?
> Shall I give my first-born for my transgression,
>   the fruit of my body for the sin of my soul?"

Note the progression to a climax from burnt offerings, calves, rams, oil, to the offering of a first-born child! Then the priest answers, summarizing what it is that the Lord really wants:

> He has showed you, O man, what is good;
>   and what does the LORD require of you
> but to do justice [mišpāṭ], and to love kindness,
>   and to walk humbly with your God?

Again, in the prophetic way of speaking, justice is something one does, involving dynamic activity. In those sermons where the two terms are used together, justice and righteousness denote the *results* of this activity. Thus these qualities once filled Jerusalem (1:21), are absent in the prophet's time (5:7) but will again be present during the rule of the Messiah (9:7) in the new Jerusalem (28:17).

Secondly, Isaiah understands doing justice as the *response* of the People of God to what God has done for them. This is clear from the Song of the Vineyard. Remember for a moment the reminder/response structure of the Sinai covenant, as we noted it in the Ten Commandments.[2] We see the same structure here. The singer reminds his hearers of all that the vineyard keeper had done to establish the vineyard (digged it, cleared it, planted it, built a watchtower, hewed out a wine vat). And he continued to care for the vineyard day by day (5:6 assumes regular pruning and hoeing). "Remember that this is the way God has acted toward his people," said the prophet, "like a farmer patiently nurturing his vineyard!" And as the farmer expected the vineyard to produce good fruits in response to his efforts, so the Lord expected his people to respond with the "fruits" of justice and righteousness.

But of whom does God expect this response? As we continue listening to the prophet's sermons where these words occur, we discover that special responsibility lies with those in positions of political power. Rulers are exhorted to do justice for the orphan (1:17; cf. 1:10) and princes are accused as guilty when they fail to do so (1:23b). When the Messianic King comes, he will rule with justice and righteousness (9:7) and will judge (the verb šāpaṭ) the poor with righteousness (11:4). But all of the people share in this responsibility. The imperatives at the end of the sermon in 1:10–17 are addressed to the people as well as the rulers (cf. 1:10):

> seek justice, correct oppression,
> do justice for the orphan, take up the cause of the widow.

And all of the citizens are called to account when there has been a general failure to produce justice and righteousness in a society (5:3).

Finally, as we listen to Isaiah's preaching we discover that doing justice means taking up the role of *advocate* for the powerless. In these sermons about justice and righteousness we keep running into people, specifically the widow (1:17; 1:23; 10:2), the orphan (1:17; 1:23; 10:2), and the poor (3:14 f.; 10:2). This familiar trio is representative of the powerless, and in the Judah of Isaiah's day just as in the Israel of Amos' day, they are easy prey for the unscrupulous land grabber (5:8), they are not represented when legislation unfavorable to them is passed (10:1 f.), and they generally do not get a fair shake in the courts of the land (1:23; 5:23; 10:2). To do justice means to take up the cause of these people, to act as their advocate. People and political leaders alike are exhorted to do so (1:17) and the failure of leadership to act as advocate for the powerless has caused once faithful Jerusalem to become a faithless whore of a city (1:21–23).

WHEN JUSTICE IS NOT DONE

What happens when a people and their leaders fail to do justice, when they exploit and oppress the powerless, rather than act as their advocates? On occasion, the prophet could simply pronounce a woe over such a nation, signaling that there was a funeral in their near future (5:22 f.; 10:1 f.). But the prophet also announced that these powerless were not left without an advocate. The cry that resounded through the streets of Jerusalem in place of the righteousness that should have been there (5:7) was a cry heard before God (cf. Exod. 22:22–24)! If the courts of Judah would not hear the cases of the widow, the orphan, and the poor, another court would— no less than the heavenly court of the Lord himself! On one occasion Isaiah addressed political leaders in language which reminded them of the instruction they had received from their teachers in Jerusalem:

> Do not rob the poor, because he is poor,
>   or crush the afflicted at the gate;
> for the LORD will plead their cause,
>   and despoil of life those who despoil them.
>   (Prov. 22:22 f.)[3]

Now he announced that the case of the People vs. the Administration had come to a higher court! And it was God himself who was acting as Advocate for the people:

> The LORD has taken his place to make an accusation,
>   he stands to judge nations.
> The LORD comes with a case [mišpāṭ]
>   against the elders and princes of his people:
> "It is you who have devoured the vineyard,
>   the spoil of the poor is in your houses.
> What do you mean by crushing my people,
>   by grinding the face of the poor?"
>   says the Lord God of hosts.
>   (3:13–15, my translation)

A city, a nation which has failed to do justice by failing in the role of advocate for the powerless was a city and nation which had to face the accusation of God in his Supreme Court. On another occasion the prophet announced the sentence of that Court. The community so filled with corruption would have to face the fires of God's judgment (1:24–26). The land where concern for the powerless had been replaced by the cries of the oppressed would be a land left a wasteland (5:5 f.).

But this was not the prophet's last word. There remained a future for this people, beyond the coming tragedy, and in that future lasting justice and righteousness would be established. The speech in 1:21–26 announced that the coming doom would be a purging and refining process, and after the purge the city would again be called the "city of righteousness, the faithful city." Much the same thought is expressed in the sermon found in Isaiah 28:14–22. At a time when the rulers of the nations were plotting a course which seemed to the prophet to be one of national suicide, he announced that after the storm of judgment, God would build a new city, employing justice and righteousness as the very standards for its construction (28:17). But the sayings about the Messiah speak the most clearly about the future hopes. Speaking to a Judah experiencing the ravages of a war with Syria and Israel, the prophet portrayed a future time when the administration of the Davidic king would be marked by lasting peace, justice, and righteousness (9:7). And on another occasion as he described the rule of a new son of Jesse, a "New David," he described him in the role of advocate for the powerless: " . . . but with righteousness he shall judge [verb, šāpaṭ] the poor, and decide with equity for the meek of the earth." (11:4a)

We might summarize what we have learned about "doing justice" as follows:

1. Doing justice in the prophetic style means the People of God responding to what God has done for them.

2. This response involves taking up the role of advocates for the powerless.

3. God himself acts as Advocate for the powerless, and will finally establish justice and righteousness through his Messiah.

TAKING UP THE ADVOCATE ROLE

But what does the prophetic preaching mean for us? We suggest that these summary statements can provide guidelines as we seek to work for justice in our own time.

1. Who are the People of God today? We have already seen that, according to the New Testament, those who call themselves Christians are the New Israel, the New People of God. Most of the time these people are scattered throughout the world, going about their work as farmers, teachers, doctors, nurses, carpenters, housewives, or whatever. But week by week they gather to worship, and there they are reminded of what God has done for them. Did the prophets remind their audiences of the Exodus? We hear about it too, but this time it is a New Exodus, brought about by the work of Jesus Christ, and resulting in deliverance not from any political power like Egypt, but from sin, death, and the power of the devil. Did the prophets remind their hearers of the covenant relationship? We are reminded of a New Covenant established in an upper room (1 Cor. 11:23–26) and reaffirmed each time the Lord's Supper is celebrated. And we are also reminded of the everyday good gifts that a loving heavenly father gives to us, like "food and clothing, home and family, daily work, and all I need from day to day."[4]

God has done much for us and given us much. But what of our response? The vineyard keeper expected some good fruits. And we have learned, following Paul and the reformers, to speak of good works as "fruits of faith." Jesus taught that much would be expected from those who have been given much (Luke 12:48). Notice how often Paul's letters begin with a reminder of what God has done (Romans 1–11; Ephesians 1–3) and then continue by giving directives for the expected response (Romans 12–15; Ephesians 4–6). Luther put it this way: "It is true that we are justified by faith alone without works, but I speak of the true faith which after it justifies does not snore lazily, but is active in love."[5]

Perhaps you have been involved in congregational discussions when it is time to call a new pastor. "We want a pastor who will stick to preaching the Gospel!" some will say. Others will counter, "We want someone who will get us involved in the great social issues of our day!" Isaiah's Song of the Vineyard can help us to keep straight the relationship between the Gospel and social involvement. The preaching of the Good News, proclaiming what God has done, is always primary. But God expects a response from those who hear the Good News. He wants a people whose faith is not lazy and snoring, but active in love (Gal. 5:6). God has acted in Christ to set us free; to that action, he expects a reaction. We sometimes speak of "Christian social action." More accurately, we should describe such efforts as "Christian social reaction," the People of God reacting by trying to help the hurts of the world, loving "because he first loved us." (1 John 4:19)

2. But what form should this reaction take? To be sure, the prophets provide us with no specific answers as to how we should vote on abortion, housing, busing, tax reform, or the like. Nor does the Bible furnish us with any blueprints or programs for social welfare. But one thing is clear. If we as a People of God are interested in doing justice in the prophetic style, we are asked to act as advocates for the powerless, lobbyists for those who have no clout in the public arena.

And so it would seem that the question for us is: Who are the powerless in our time and our place? What about the young Indian girl involved in an accidental shooting, now waiting for her day in court? Will she get a fair trial? Or the old widower whose landlord keeps raising the rent and refusing to repair the heating system? What about the confused high school junior whose parents have disowned her because she is pregnant? Who is watching out for her? And what about that child yet to be born, a "powerless" one who needs an advocate in the worst way? And then there is the factory worker who has been laid off, and has received an eviction notice because he can't pay the rent. Who cares about him and his hungry children? The biblical statement that we shall always have the poor with us (John 12:8) is often quoted; the prophet asks whether the poor will have us *with* them, acting as their advocates.

Lest sensitive Christian people fear involvement in social causes at the expense of our calling to communicate the gospel, let us remember that often the most effective kind of communication is non-verbal. Peter Berger tells about an old priest working in the slums of a European city. When asked why he was doing it, he said " 'So that the rumour of God may not disappear completely.' "[6] His was an eloquent proclamation of the gospel, a love not confined to "word or speech but in deed and in truth." (1 John 3:18) I recall from seminary days an occasional assignment at a mission in the heart of the city slums. In this mission, the men had to listen to our sermons before they got a bowl of soup. No sermon, no soup. In the mission down the street, the soup was offered with no sermonic strings attached. It may be that the other mission communicated the gospel more effectively than we did; it is difficult to concentrate on preaching (especially from seminarians) on an empty stomach! But a People of God interested in really *doing* justice in the prophetic style would not offer just soup, with or without a sermon, but would also be trying to act as advocates for these men, lobbying for them in the public arena to try to aid them in putting their broken lives back together again.

3. What does it mean to say that God himself acts as Advocate for the powerless? Isaiah portrayed God as taking

up the cause of the poor in the heavenly courtroom (Isa. 3:13–15). But something has happened since the time of Isaiah. God the Advocate has come down to earth. The advocate role has become a reality, in the flesh and blood of Jesus of Nazareth. Notice the attitude and actions of Jesus toward the widow (Luke 7:11–17; 21:1–4), the poor (Luke 6:20; 14:12–14), and those whom society rejects (Luke 7:36–50; 15). Jesus is the Advocate, the Man *for* Others. Thus his arrival on the scene comes as good news for the powerless—the poor, captive, blind, and oppressed (Luke 4:18).

The New Testament is like a news report, announcing, "Now is the hour!" Isaiah's Prince of Peace has been born and rules with justice and righteousness, it says! The New David has appeared, going about his ministry with special concern for the poor and the meek! The date in the corner of the checks you write and on the license plate of the car you drive testifies that almost two thousand years ago something happened which has changed things on this planet ever since.

But along with the New Testament "now" there is a "not yet." There remain some promises to be fulfilled. Widows continue to weep, orphans go hungry, and the poor we still have with us, as Jesus himself said (Mark 14:7). The world still hurts, and God's people look forward to the day when his kingdom will be perfectly established and he will wipe away every tear (Rev. 7:17). But until that time, we live by the Good News that

> . . . we have an advocate with the Father, Jesus Christ the righteous; and he is the expiation for our sins, and not for ours only but also for the sins of the whole world. (1 John 2:1–2)

As he was Messiah and the Man for Others, we who call ourselves Messiah's people (that is what "Christians" really means) are called to be a People for Others. Our calling is to respond to the Good News by acting as advocates for the powerless.

7

Who Are the Prophets for Our Time?

Now we return to the question raised at the end of our first chapter. Are there prophets today? Who are the Elijahs, Amoses, or Isaiahs who can bring a Word from God to us, in our time?

THE TIME OF THE PROPHETS

I remember a conversation in my office with a student from the first college class in Bible that I taught. He, a freshman, came in to tell me that he was quite disappointed with the course. He had expected that studying religion would be something quite different. "This course in Bible," he said, "is too much like a history course." I don't recall how I answered him then. But now, after a decade of teaching, I know what I would say. I would tell him that the course in Bible is so much like a history course because the Bible is so much like a history book. There is a story about a small boy who somewhat fearfully entered a large library and asked at the desk for a book about penguins. When the librarian returned with a huge volume on the subject, his reply was, "That's more than I want to know about penguins!" My freshman student, from whom I learned something, was saying that his introductory Bible course had provided him with more than he wanted to know about Jeroboam II or Tiglath-pileser III! Yet, I hope that he, and you the reader also, discovered for himself in listening to the preaching of Amos or Isaiah that if we are going to understand the prophets at all, we need to hear them first in their own time.

The prophets also lived and worked in certain places, with names like Israel or Judah, Bethel or Jerusalem. Even inexpensive editions of the Bible usually include a few maps among the last pages. Perhaps these are not often used, but they serve as reminders that the Bible tells about events that happened in real places and which can be located on real maps. One time I met a bookseller in Jerusalem who had published a very useful atlas of modern Israel. I asked how he had come to be so interested in geography. He said that he had grown up in a little village in Germany, and had gone one time to mail a letter to a relative in Jerusalem. The postmaster looked at him in astonishment and simply handed the letter back. "You can't mail this," he said. "There is no such place as Jerusalem—that's only in the Bible!" And so, said the bookseller, he wanted everyone to know everything about Jerusalem and Israel, the height of the mountains, the depth of the seas, the populations of the cities and villages. I hope that you have also sensed as we have listened together to the voices of the prophets that they lived and worked in real places, in towns and villages where old men and old women sat, and where boys and girls played in the streets.

The prophets had their times, and their places. We have already noted that the time of the prophets ran alongside the time of the kings.[1] The age of prophecy had a beginning, with Samuel, and it came to an end, sometime after the monarchy was through. The Old Testament itself recognizes that the time of the great prophets came to an end. Psalm 74, written after the destruction of Jerusalem, declares, "We do not see our signs; there is no longer any prophet." (vs. 9)

THE TIME OF THE SON

The New Testament also acknowledges that prophecy had its special time. The Letter to the Hebrews begins:

> In many and various ways God spoke of old to our fathers by the prophets; but in these last days he has spoken to us by a Son. . . .(Heb. 1:1 f.)

There was a time when God communicated with his people by sending his word through his messengers, the prophets. But now, says the author of Hebrews, God has communicated with us by sending his Son, in the person of Jesus from Nazareth.

Who was this Jesus? When he interrupted a funeral procession to bring a young boy back to life, the crowd could only conclude that " 'A great prophet has risen among us!' " (Luke 7:16) He did the kinds of things the prophets used to do. And he preached like the prophets too. We have listened to Nathan's parable about the ewe lamb and Isaiah's song-parable about a vineyard. When Jesus used parables, he must have reminded his hearers of the prophets. He preached words of woe with all the fire of an Amos or an Isaiah (Matt. 23). But he could preach words of comfort, too (Matt. 5:3–12), as the prophets before him had done (Isa. 40–55, for example). Jesus acted and spoke like the prophets of old, and when he entered Jerusalem at the end of his career, the crowds called him " ' . . . the prophet Jesus from Nazareth of Galilee.' " (Matt. 21:11)

A prophet? Yes, but more than a prophet. The prophets introduced their messages with "Thus says the Lord," identifying God as the source and authority for what they said; Jesus said, " 'You have heard that it was said to the men of old . . . *but I say to you*,' " claiming himself as source and authority for what he had to say (Matt. 5:21–48). The prophets promised a Messiah from the line of David (Isa. 9, 11; Micah 5:2–6; Zech. 9:9–10); the New Testament announces that

Jesus is that Messiah or, to use the Greek word for Messiah, the Christ (Mark 8:27–30; 14:61 f., as examples).[2] The prophet speaks of a Servant of the Lord who will accomplish his mission through suffering (Isa. 42:1–4; 49:1–6; 50:4–11; 52:13–53:12); the New Testament identifies Jesus as the one whose life, death, and resurrection followed the Servant pattern (the Gospels), as the one who "emptied himself, taking the form of a servant" (Phil. 2:5–11), and as the person about whom Isaiah 52–53 was speaking (Acts 8:26–35).

Who is this Jesus? The New Testament piles title upon title to answer that question—Son of God, Prophet, Messiah, Servant, Son of Man, Rabbi, Lamb of God, the list goes on and on. As we read that book, one thing is certain. With the life, death, and resurrection of Jesus, the old promises were fulfilled. Peter said it: " . . . all the prophets who have spoken, from Samuel and those who came afterwards, also proclaimed these days." (Acts 3:24) Paul wrote it: " . . . all the promises of God find their Yes in him." (2 Cor. 1:20) The time of the Son was a new time, a time when God was saying something to the world in a new way. This time his Word did not come through his messengers the prophets, but that Word took on human form in the person of Jesus (John 1:14). And the message to the world was clear. When God raised Jesus from the dead, the powers of sin, death, and the devil were defeated. That was—and is—Good News, and the People of God have been preaching it ever since.

OUR TIME

Finally, what shall we say about our time, almost two thousand years after the time of Jesus? And about our place, just past the two-hundredth anniversary of the birth of our nation?

As we look back over the past decades, we might describe the fifties as the decade of technological advance, symbolized in the satellite Sputnik orbiting our planet. In the sixties, the great concerns within our nation were sociological, with the freedom marches and civil rights movement, and also political, as we agonized over the war in Vietnam. As the seventies began, we were awakened to ecological issues and began working in earnest to conserve our natural resources. And now, moving toward the eighties, it seems that there is a new interest in the realm of the spiritual. People are reading books about the occult and watching movies about demon possession and exorcism. In the high schools, students are requesting from their teachers courses in religion and the Bible. College students are "into" Eastern religions in a way which we have not seen before. There are seers, diviners, mystics, and mediums to spare! Some call themselves prophets, and offer predictions on everything from the weather to politics. Within the church, there is a rediscovery of the Holy Spirit in the charismatic movement. Thus at the time of our nation's bicentennial, we seem to have moved from technological concerns through those which are sociological, political, ecological, and now essentially theological. That slogan "the Spirit of '76" may turn out to express the rediscovery of the dimension of the spiritual in our nation at the time of its two-hundredth anniversary.

But where can we look for guidance, in the midst of this highly charged spiritual atmosphere of the seventies? Where can we listen for a Word which will help us to find our way? Who are the prophets for our time?

In our opening chapter, we learned something about figures like Black Elk, Edgar Cayce, and Jeane Dixon. No doubt others like them will continue to see visions, hear voices, and make predictions, with greater or lesser degrees of accuracy and authenticity. We argued that these individuals ought to be called "seers," and tried to point out that they are examples of a class of unique persons who have appeared all over the world and throughout history. As we compared the biblical prophets to them, we discovered that there was something of the seer in the prophet. But a prophet was more than a seer, and a seer was not—and is not—a prophet. Individuals like these, we conclude, are not the prophets for our time.

Our investigation has focused on what certain of the biblical prophets had to say in their preaching about the powerless. As we reflect on the question, "Who are the prophets for our time?" we think of contemporary individuals who have acted as advocates for the powerless in an especially effective manner. Names like Reinhold Niebuhr, Martin Luther King, Jr., and Abraham Heschel come to mind—the reader can add others as well. These men preached and acted in ways which are reminiscent of the biblical prophets. Who can forget the resounding cadences of Martin Luther King, Jr.'s, "I Have a Dream" sermon, or the inspiring sight of the bearded Rabbi Heschel marching in the forefront of the civil rights and anti-war marches? Through their words and actions, these men called a community or a nation to take up the cause of the powerless. Shall we then call them prophets? Are they among the prophets for our time? Again, our study suggests a negative answer to these questions. These individuals spoke and acted *like* the biblical prophets, and they drew their inspiration *from* the biblical prophets. In this sense their lives and words may be called "prophetic." But this does not mean that they *were* prophets and they themselves did not claim to be such.

Then who are the prophets for today? Who are the Elijahs, the Amoses and the Isaiahs for our time? They are—Elijah, Amos, Isaiah, and the rest of that company of prophets whom we discover in the Bible! Lest the reader think that this is an attempt at a clever or pious dodge of the question, allow me to explain.

We have been arguing that the Bible takes time and history seriously. The writer of Ecclesiastes reminds us that "For everything there is a season, and a time for every matter under heaven." (Eccl. 3:1) Every Christian understands that there was a time when God was present among men in a special way. We have called this the time of the Son. Christian preaching focuses on the events of this unique time, proclaiming the Good News about what God did through the life, death, and resurrection of Jesus Christ. Christian teaching draws from the words of Jesus and of the disciples and apostles, seeking to interpret and apply them to our own time. Are there "disciples and apostles" today? On occasion, we might use these terms to describe present-day Christians. But we recognize that *the* disciples and *the* apostles were a special group, who happened to live at the time of the Son and whose witness we find recorded in the New Testament.

The situation is the same with the prophets. There was a time when God communicated with men in a special way. This we have called the time of the prophets; it was a time with a beginning and an end, which roughly corresponded with the period of the monarchy in ancient Israel and Judah. We discovered that in order to understand the words of these prophets, we had to begin by learning something about the time in which they lived. We must listen to them first of all in their own historical and geographical setting. But as we listen, we discover that their words refuse to be confined to these times and places. These words have a power about them, and because of this power the People of God have remembered them, written them down, and have continued to hear through them a Word from God, accusing, comforting, and giving direction. We discover that the God of our fathers continues to speak to us through Elijah, Amos, Isaiah and all the rest, if we will but listen for his Word through their words as we find them written in the Old Testament.

These prophets call a People of God who have been radically loved to become radical lovers of the powerless. They warn us against the arrogance that tends to accompany national or individual power and alert us to the indifference that accompanies affluence. I once heard it said of a carpenter that he built his Christianity into his houses; the prophets remind us that true religion is like that, not kept in a compartment, but permeating all of life. Finally, the prophets call us to be advocates, lobbyists for those who are powerless in our time.

In such ways God spoke of old to our fathers by the prophets; in such ways he continues to speak to us through those same prophets today.

Notes

PREFACE

1 The following books were mentioned; the reader can extend the list by a tour through any bookstore: Ruth Montgomery, *A Gift of Prophecy: The Phenomenal Jeane Dixon*. New York: Bantam Books, Inc., 1966.

Jeane Dixon, *My Life and Prophecies*. New York: Bantam Books Inc., 1970.

Jeane Dixon, *The Call to Glory: Jeane Dixon Speaks of Jesus and Prophecy*. New York: Bantam Books Inc., 1973.

Jess Stearn, *Edgar Cayce—The Sleeping Prophet*. New York: Bantam Books Inc., 1968.

Erich von Däniken, *Chariots of the Gods? Unsolved Mysteries of the Past*. Translated by Michael Heron. New York: Bantam Books Inc., 1971.

Josef F. Blumrich, *The Spaceships of Ezekiel*. New York: Bantam Books Inc., 1973.

Hal Lindsey with C. C. Carlson, *The Late Great Planet Earth*. Grand Rapids: Zondervan Publishing House, 1970.

Hal Lindsey, *There's a New World Coming*. Santa Ana: Vision House Publishers, 1973.

CHAPTER 1: WHAT WAS A PROPHET?

1 Jess Stearn, *Edgar Cayce—The Sleeping Prophet*, p. 27.

2 *Ibid.*, p. 131.

3 Ruth Montgomery, *A Gift of Prophecy*, p. ix.

4 *Ibid.*, p. 17.

5 *Ibid.*, p. 169.

6 Jeane Dixon, *The Call to Glory*, p. 34.

7 John G. Neihardt, *Black Elk Speaks* (Lincoln: University of Nebraska Press, 1961), Chapter III, pp. 20–47.

8 *Ibid.*, Chapter XX, pp. 228–233.

9 *Ibid.*, pp. 208–209.

10 *Ibid.*, p. 277.

11 From *Prophecy in Ancient Israel* by Johannes Lindblom, (Philadelphia: Fortress Press, 1962), pp. 83–84. Reprinted with permission of the publisher.

CHAPTER 2: INTERPRETING THE PROPHETS

1 Lindsey, p. 93.

2 *Ibid.*, p. 94.

3 *Ibid.*, p. 93; chapter 9.

4 *Ibid.*, pp. 151f.
5 Von Däniken, p. 37.
6 *Ibid.*, pp. 37f., quoting Ezek. 1:4–7.
7 *Ibid.*, p. 38.
8 For an illustration, see the article "Angel" by T. H. Gaster, in *The Interpreter's Dictionary of the Bible* (New York: Abingdon Press, 1962), Vol. I, p. 132.
9 Von Däniken, p. 38.
10 *Ibid.*, pp. 38ff.

CHAPTER 3: THE POWERLESS

1 See the discussion below, p. 42
2 See the discussion below, pp. 42–44.
3 William Stringfellow, *A Private and Public Faith* (Grand Rapids: William B. Eerdmans Publishing Company, 1962), pp. 78–79. Used by permission.

CHAPTER 4: THE ARROGANCE OF POWER

1 For these texts, see James B. Pritchard, editor, *Ancient Near Eastern Texts Relating to the Old Testament* (Princeton: Princeton University Press, 2nd ed., 1955), pp. 412ff. For a good commentary on them, see R. B. Y. Scott, *Proverbs and Ecclesiastes, The Anchor Bible*, vol. 18 (Garden City: Doubleday and Company, Inc., 1967), pp. xl–xlv.
2 Søren Kierkegaard, *For Self-Examination*, translated by Edna and Howard Hong (Minneapolis: Augsburg Publishing House, 1940), pp. 41–42. Note the masterful exposition of this whole incident.

CHAPTER 5: AMOS AND THE AFFLUENT SOCIETY

1 See James Luther Mays, *Amos* (Philadelphia: The Westminster Press, 1969), p. 20.
2 John Bright, *A History of Israel* (Philadelphia: The Westminster Press, second edition, 1972), p. 255.
3 *Service Book and Hymnal of the Lutheran Church in America* (Minneapolis: Augsburg, 1958), p. 104.
4 For a full discussion see Mays, pp. 90 ff. Note that the *New American Bible* rearranges the verses in the sequence 6, 8, 9, 7, 10, 11.
5 For this "woe" translation, see Mays, pp. 90 f.;note also the *New American Bible*.
6 See Mays, p. 115.

CHAPTER 6: ADVOCATES FOR THE POWERLESS

1 The translation of verse 1 is my own; the remainder follows the Revised Standard Version.

2   See pp. 26–28 above.

3   See pp. 31–35 above.

4   Luther's explanation to the first article of the Apostle's Creed, *The Small Catechism* (Minneapolis: Augsburg Publishing House, 1960), p. 10.

5   Quoted by George Wolfgang Forell, *Faith Active in Love* (Minneapolis: Augsburg Publishing House, 1954), p. 89.

6   Peter L. Berger, *A Rumor of Angels* (Garden City: Doubleday and Company, Inc., 1970), pp. 94 f.

CHAPTER 7: WHO ARE THE PROPHETS FOR OUR TIME?

1   See above, p. 40.

2   The *Today's English Version* of the New Testament (*Good News for Modern Man*) ordinarily translates the Greek *Christos* as "Messiah"; see these references from Mark's Gospel.

Selected Bibliography

THE BIBLE

The New Oxford Annotated Bible with the Apocrypha, edited by Herbert G. May and Bruce M. Metzger (New York: Oxford, 1973). The Revised Standard Version, plus articles, maps, and helpful comments at the bottom of each page.

BIBLE DICTIONARY AND COMMENTARIES ON THE WHOLE BIBLE

The Interpreter's Dictionary of the Bible, in 4 vols., edited by George Arthur Buttrick and others (New York: Abingdon, 1962). Articles on names, places, theological themes.

The Layman's Bible Commentary, in 25 vols., edited by Balmer H. Kelly (Richmond: John Knox, 1959). Reliable and readable.

Peake's Commentary on the Bible, edited by Matthew Black and H. H. Rowley (New York: Nelson, 1962). Note especially the article, "Old Testament Prophecy" by James Muilenburg, and the treatment of Isaiah 1–39 by John Bright.

BOOKS

Bright, John, *A History of Israel* (Philad phia: Westminster, 2nd edition, 1972). Indispensable for understanding the prophets in their own time.

Bright, John, *The Kingdom of God* (New York: Abingdon, 1953). On the whole Bible, but particularly valuable on the prophets.

Bright, John, *Jeremiah*, in *The Anchor Bible*, Vol. 21 (Garden City: Doubleday, 1965). Note especially the introductory article, "The Prophets of Israel: Some Preliminary Remarks."

Mays, James Luther, *Amos*, in *The Old Testament Library* (Philadelphia: Westminster, 1969). Particularly helpful in understanding the various forms of prophetic speech.

von Rad, Gerhard, *Old Testament Theology*, Vol. 2, translated by D. M. G. Stalker (New York: Harper and Row, 1965). One of the giants; begins with a masterful introduction to prophecy.

Westermann, Claus, *Handbook to the Old Testament*, translated and edited by Robert H. Boyd (Minneapolis: Augsburg, 1967). Outlines the structure of each book of the Old Testament.

Westermann, Claus, *A Thousand Years and a Day*, translated by Stanley Rudman (Philadelphia: Fortress, 1962). Fresh consideration of the importance of the Old Testament and the prophets for our time.

Wolff, Hans Walter, *The Old Testament: A Guide to Its Writings*, translated by Keith R. Crim (Philadelphia: Fortress, 1973). Short introduction to the whole Old Testament; includes an excellent discussion of the prophetic books.

PERIODICALS

The Biblical Archaeologist, edited by Edward F. Campbell, Jr., and H. Darrell Lance (Cambridge, Mass.: The American Schools of Oriental Research). Reports on the implications of current archaeological work for biblical study.

Interpretation, edited by James L. Mays (Richmond: Union Theological Seminary in Virginia). Articles on biblical and theological themes, along with reviews of current literature on the Bible.